ELTON JOHN
and Bernie Taupin

is a Star Original

Paul Gambaccini got it all together, so you have
him to thank. Born in 1949, he has attended Dart-
mouth College and Oxford University, managed a
commercial radio station, edited for *Rolling Stone*,
appeared on BBC Radios One and Four, written
a column for the *New Musical Express*, broadcast on
UPI's Audio Network, and interviewed Richard
Nixon, Paul McCartney, and a man who played
'William Tell' on his head.

ELTON JOHN

and Bernie Taupin

A STAR BOOK

published by
W. H. ALLEN

A Star Book
Published in 1975
by W. H. Allen & Co. Ltd.
A division of Howard & Wyndham Ltd.
44 Hill Street, London W1X 8LB

Printed in Great Britain by
Richard Clay (The Chaucer Press) Ltd, Bungay, Suffolk

ISBN 0 352 30058 2

Portions of this book appeared in *Rolling Stone* No. 141.

To Helen, Penny and Caroline

ELTON JOHN

ELTON: Actually it all started when I became old enough to listen to records, because my mother and father collected records and the first records I ever heard were Kay Starr and Billy May and Tennessee Ernie Ford and Les Paul and Mary Ford and Guy Mitchell. I grew up in that era. I was three or four when I first started listening to records like that. I obviously took a great interest in them, and then I went through the skiffle thing with Lonnie Donegan. The first records my mom brought home that I was really knocked out by were "Hound Dog", and "ABC Boogie" by Bill Haley. That changed my life, I couldn't believe it. So my parents really influenced me by just having music around all the time. Then rock and roll really changed my life. I heard Little Richard and Jerry Lee Lewis and that was it. I didn't ever want to be anything else. I just started banging away and sort of semi-studied classical music at the Royal Academy of Music but sort of half-heartedly. I was never really interested in it. Bluesology got together when I was about fourteen, playing in scout huts and youth club dances. Just one ten-watt amplifier with the piano unamplified.

We started off by playing . . . we started off by playing . . . (annoyed) I can *never* remember what we started off by playing . . . gradually we got into playing Jimmy Witherspoon numbers, we were always playing the wrong stuff. Bluesology were always two months too late, or three years too early, never playing the right thing at the right time. They were always appealing to minority tastes. We always thought we were hip because we were playing Jimmy Witherspoon songs. It sounds ludicrous, and Mose Allison numbers, but they were sort of the hip figures of that era. It was the time of Georgie Fame and the Blue Flames. What was that classic Ray Charles thing (sings piano part) . . . "Let the Good Times Roll", things like that. Then we started to add brass, because brass was the thing.

Then we went for an audition at the State Cinema at Kilburn on a Saturday morning. There were thousands of groups and you had to play two or three numbers. The guy there from the agency, the Roy Tempest Agency, I don't know where he ever disappeared to, asked if we would be interested in turning professional and backing all these American people. Backing Major Lance was probably the biggest thing that ever happened to me. So we said yes, originally it was going to be Wilson Pickett but his guitarist didn't like the band. The first person I ever played for really as a professional was Major Lance although when we turned professional I was working at a music publisher's taking tea around and packing the parcels. While I was in school I was playing in a pub every Friday, Saturday and Sunday night for a year. This was all to earn money to buy electric pianos and mikes and amplifiers and things. I used to make a quid a night but then I'd take my box around and people would put donations in it. For my age, I was making a fortune, getting about thirty-five quid a week, I think.

But it was Major Lance who was the first person in our lives, and from then on it was a succession of people. Patti LaBelle twice——

PG: Mention the Blue Bellies.

ELTON: There were clubs we played in you never heard of, and there were posters outside like "Tonight, The Fantastic Patti LaBelle and Her Blue Bellies". I mean, some of these places you would just not believe. We never had road managers in those days. The artists who came over, it was really like a slave camp. There was one day with Billy Stewart we started out playing an American serviceman's club in London, finished that at four, raced up to Birmingham, played there, and came back to Paddington [London train station] and played there the same night. At the time we didn't think anything of it, taking our equipment up and down the stairs. We used to really work our ass off. Looking back on it, it was the most miserable existence, but at the time it was quite happy. We backed . . . let's see . . . Patti LaBelle twice, the Original Drifters for two gigs, we did a whole tour with Doris Troy, and a whole tour with the Ink Spots (laughter), and Billy Stewart. In between not working, by that I mean not backing people, we did the traditional months in Hamburg. That was another thing that changed my life and made me grow up. Then we went to Sweden and then the south of France for a month. We just did mediocre things. We never starved, but it was such a mundane experience. We were doing all those soul numbers. I remember seeing the Move in Birmingham, I was sitting in the back row, and saying they were going to make it. I always wanted to make it, you see. That wasn't good enough, I used to get so depressed. Sure enough, they made it, the Move, you used to see other people coming up and you'd think, here I am, plodding on. I really got pissed off.

Then when John Baldry came along and said would you like to join up I said well, at least it's a step in the right direction. So we backed John for a year, starting off with a soul package, really. It was our singer, who was Stuart A. Brown, Marsha Hunt, another singer called Alan Walker, and Baldry. Baldry had just finished with the Brian Auger thing, and Julie Driscoll, the Steampacket, with Rod Stewart, and he wanted to start another similar thing. It really didn't ever get off the ground, we were never a success, so Baldry decided to make a commercial record and made a hit record with "Let the Heartaches Begin". That changed his life for two or three years and began to change mine, because it meant instead of playing in clubs you played in cabaret, which really drove me around the bend. I think that's the graveyard of musicians, playing cabaret. I think I'd rather be dead than work in cabaret.

So I was always getting depressed and it was in Newcastle that I saw the advert in the *New Musical Express* saying "Liberty leaving EMI, going independent, need singers and talent". I didn't know what I was going to do, I just knew I wanted to come off the road. So I went up for an appointment, I was still with the band. I said I can't write lyrics and I can't really sing well because I wasn't singing with Bluesology, but I think I can write songs. So they gave me this audition, it was in a recording studio, they said "sing us five songs". I didn't know five songs, all I knew were the songs Baldry was singing and the Jim Reeves records I used to sing with at home. So I sang five Jim Reeves songs and they turned me down flat. I don't really blame them. They put me in touch with Bernie, only through letter or by phone, because Liberty didn't want us.

But some guy at Liberty named Ray Williams told me to go to Dick James Music and do some demos. I was receiving Bernie's lyrics and writing the songs and doing demos before I even met Bernie. One day I was doing a demo session and noticed him in the corner. I said oh, are you the lyric writer, and he said, "yeah", and we went around the corner for a cup of coffee and that was it, really.

9

We'd made millions and millions of songs up before anybody discovered we were making demos at Dick James. Dick James had a purge because he discovered that people were using his studios just to make endless demos. So he heard our stuff, liked it, and signed us up. As soon as he signed us up at ten quid a week advance royalties I left the group. That was the best day in my life, when I quit the group.

PG: Was it then he suggested the name change?

ELTON: Oh, no, I was coming back from Scotland, or somewhere, after doing a gig with John and Caleb Quavle, who was engineer at the Dick James Studio at the time, and had a lot to do with my early encouragement and played the guitar for Baldry some of the time, with Bluesology, and I said, I've got to think of a name, I'm fed up with Reg Dwight, I can't be Reg Dwight if I'm going to be a singer, so I've got to think of a name. So Elton Dean's name I pinched [Elton Dean was in Bluesology and later the Soft Machine] and John Baldry's name and I said, oh, Elton John, there you go.

BERNIE TAUPIN

BERNIE: That whole thing about us getting together is that when we were first asked it, we told everybody the full story, very long and very technical, and then as time went on we started cutting it down and it got shorter and shorter and shorter until finally we had a condensed version of how we got together, leaving out all the horrible little teeny fragments. Somebody asked me just the other night and I didn't know what to say. I just gulped and ran out of the room, I couldn't stand the thought of going through all that. All the ins and outs, and the newspaper advert, and . . . uhhhhh . . .

PG: The classic part is your mother taking the letter out of the wastebasket.

BERNIE: That's sort of like a fairy tale, isn't it? It didn't happen like that, it wasn't like "Oh, what's this letter my son has thrown into the garbage? A letter! I must post it!" She probably said "you should do it, you should do it," but it was never a matter of grappling with the garbage.

PG: What had you been doing before that?

BERNIE: I left school when I was sixteen and went to work as an apprentice in a printer's, for a local paper.

11

When I told the employment office I wanted to work on a paper it wasn't exactly in the machine room! Sort of more "ace reporter", you know, but I ended up in the machine room, unfortunately. That drove me crazy, I couldn't stand it, it was one of those horrible Northern factory-type machine rooms with very high sky-lights, very dark and gloomy, and little men walking around asking for their sixpence a week to join the union. I just wasn't cut out for that, no way. I got fired from there in the end for trying to find another job during working hours. I spent a lot of time just doing nothing, really. I was out of work for long spells in between various jobs, I was working on farms, I ran a broiler farm, you know, a chicken farm, but I got fired from that as well. I can't remember, I must have had an argument with somebody. I enjoyed that in the time that I did it. As I said, all this was cut up with periods where I wasn't doing much, I was playing a lot of snooker and drinking a lot of beer, and staying out all night. (Laughter.) That really got on top of me in the end, just doing nothing. I got to a point where doing nothing just didn't appeal to me, I had to do something, something that I enjoyed. It was sort of like Dick Whittington, packing my little bags and trundling down to London. I came to London just after I'd written in to answer the advert, Liberty securing "talent" and all this, and I hung around London for a while, and then the whole thing came together where we met. I was still going back up north and coming back down again. Things went on from there.

PG: You told me backstage last week that at the beginning you were a little wary of how Elton would treat your lyrics. At what point did you really get confidence in him?

BERNIE: It didn't take too long. We did a lot of demos and a lot of recording even before the *Empty Sky* album was made. That material was so separated from anything we did later, we were writing very very commercial poppy songs, also pseudo-intellectual pre-flower power trash. "Mirrors of My Mind" and "Lemonade Lake" stuff, you know? Really awful. I think we were both very naive as far as writing songs and the construction of songs went. Then we got around to doing the *Empty Sky* album, which was the beginning of us being pulled together as a song-writing team. There are some really bad things on that album, some naughty things that were really bad, you know?

PG: Musically?

BERNIE: Musically, lyrically. They were very childish. Their sentiments were very trite. After that album came out we really started writing some prolific songs, songs that were worthwhile putting something behind. That was the time I really realized it was working well, that I didn't think there could be anybody else who could do it as well. It gradually got better and it was during the *Tumbleweed* album that there was no doubt about it, it was working well and had a good chance of lasting a long time. And now it just gets better and better.

PG: Do you ever suggest a mood or tempo to Elton or convey the meaning of a lyric, or does he just take them and interpret them his own way?

BERNIE: I can't remember any incidents where I've done so. The songs that I write give the idea of how they should be anyway, so it's pretty easy to pick up the mood that should suit them. I guess there may have been a couple of times when I said I had such-and-such in mind when I wrote this or such-and-such might fit, but I don't know if he takes that much notice. I give him the chance to construct it the way he wants, and I'll say if I don't think so. I know it all sounds too perfect, but that's really the way it is.

PG: Do the songs that mean the most to you generally turn out to be the ones that mean the most to him? You seem to feel that way about "Daniel", for example.

BERNIE: I think he feels more strongly about "Daniel" than I do, I like "Daniel", I think it's a good song and I think it's probably a lasting song in the same mold as "Your Song", but I wouldn't say it's my favorite song. I'd rather listen to "High Flying Bird" than "Daniel".

PG: "Crocodile Rock" turned out to be the biggest hit he ever had in America.

BERNIE: "Crocodile Rock" is in a different vein, "Daniel" is a completely different kettle of fish, a song of sentiment, whereas "Crocodile Rock" is just

14

an exuberant shit-kicker. It's very difficult because there are so many different molds our songs go into. They all belong in different categories. "Daniel" goes along with "Your Song" and "Friends" and "Tiny Dancer", whereas "Crocodile Rock" goes along with "Teacher I Need You" and "Honky Cat", the fun songs. And then there are the dramatics, like "Have Mercy on the Criminal" and possibly "Salvation", "Burn Down the Mission". So it's hard to classify what mood they're going to take.

PG: He evidently seems to like "Candle in the Wind" quite a bit, as do you.

BERNIE: Well, "Candle in the Wind" is different. "Candle in the Wind" is, I think, the best song we've ever written. I really do. It's my favorite song, it means a lot to me. I put a lot of feeling into that song, the sentiment is how I feel, and I think the melodic treatment of it really suits the mood of it. It comes across as another schmaltzy song but I believe people can listen to it and realize that the people who wrote it feel for it. I think when we actually get down to recording it it's going to be the best thing we've ever done. I think all the songs on the next album we're gonna do are going to be the best things we've ever done. We maybe say that with every album, but I feel this with this one more than I ever have before. It's got so much strong material, just so much good, enjoyable stuff.

PG: Did it bother you that Lesley Duncan's "Love Song" was included on *Tumbleweed*?

15

BERNIE: Not at all, I think it's great. I think it did a lot of good for her and I'm glad, because she needs somebody to push her. She got a lot of covers out of that, so good luck to her.

PG: How about your own album [*Taupin*]? A recent interview gave the impression you weren't satisfied with the way that had turned out and might do a second one.

BERNIE: To be quite honest, I'm not that interested in my album any more. It's gone, dead and buried. It was a thing that was fun while it was being done. I don't think I ever really made that album for the public. I made it for my own ends—well, not my own ends, that's silly to say—but for personal satisfaction. I just got a few friends, went into a studio and did some poems I wanted to get down on record. We just went in and did them, and I think the way it was done it was done well. I don't think that concept could have been done differently. It was fun while we did it and I think once it came out I forgot it. I haven't listened to that album since I did it, and I can't even remember what's on it.

PG: Well, there's the "Child" segment.

BERNIE: Yes, I think the reason I did it was because I wanted to get "Child" down. I'd written that a long time ago, when I was 17 or 18, and it just seemed it would sort of go nice on a record with some instrumentation behind it. So we just did it, and I had to fill out the other side. As it turned out, I think the other side was probably better. I think the poetry was

16

better because it was more recent. I just wanted to get it down so it was there and if I ever wanted it it was all recorded, and I could put it away and say "it's done, well I've done it now".

PG: Do you want to do another one?

BERNIE: I'd love to do another album but when I do another album it's going to be totally different. What it's going to be I have no idea, it probably won't even be poetry, I don't even know what it will be.

PG: Were you satisfied with the way *American Gothic* turned out? [Bernie produced David Ackles.]

BERNIE: Yes, very satisfied. I was more satisfied that David was satisfied with it. I think it's the only thing he's ever done he's been happy with. I don't think he's happy with his other albums, although I love them. I think the reason he liked that album so much was because I didn't tell him what to do, I just sat there and pushed him and made him do what he wanted to do, and gave him all the artistic freedom possible. He did all the arrangements, and I think that made him happy. All I did was direct from the box and give a helping hand. I was pleased with it, he was pleased with it, and I guess the public was pleased. I wish it had done better than it did. He got acclaim from it, but I think it should have gone to a wider audience. I think he'll come across one day.

PG: Will you ever work with him again?

BERNIE: Hopefully. I saw him again in Los Angeles not long ago and he'd got a whole new batch of songs together which were great. A couple of them were even commercial, believe it or not. We may have AM David Ackles yet!

PG: Any other artists you'd like to work with?

BERNIE: I love production, I love working in the studios, I love it as much as writing, really. People tend to think of me as being Bernie Taupin, lyricist for Elton John, which I guess is what I am and where my main income comes from, but I spend most of my time at home, writing for myself. I'm working on a number of projects. I just finished a children's book of poems which is being illustrated at the moment. I'm working on a marathon poem at the moment which I hope to end up being the size of a fairly good-sized book.

PG: What's it about?

BERNIE: It's very hard to explain, it's sort of on the same level of Spencer's *Fairie Queen*, where the poem ran the length of a large book. It's the same idea, it's called *The Warlord of the Marshland* and I couldn't really go into the story, it's too complicated, it's sort of a gothic story, not sort of based in any time or any space, it could be based wherever you want it to be. There's parts of everything in it. There are electronics mixed with gothic buildings. You would picture it being in the time of the Middle Ages, but in the future. The story is basically about a space of land, which is the Marshland, where there's a dying race whose ruler has just passed away. He was a very well-loved figure. He's left two sons who are identical twins and the Queen is his widow and she has to make the choice as to which of the two is to take his place. The thing is they're completely identical in all they do. They have the same level of goodness and purity in them. There's nothing different between them. She has to make the choice, and there are other forces who are trying to control one of the two. They want to get him to be chosen for their own ends.

PG: You say you spend most of your time at home. About how much of your time do you spend with Elton?

BERNIE: I don't see him as much as I used to. At one time we shared a flat together so we saw a lot of each other, but now with me living in Lincolnshire and him living down here I sort of see him whenever I come down. I guess it's not too much, really. If I move down here, I'll probably see more of him. I'd probably move up again as well!

PG: Elton says "Tiny Dancer" *is* about Maxine [Bernie's wife]. Is that true?

BERNIE: That's true, yes.

E.J. CONQUERS AMERICA

PG: Were you surprised *Elton John* really broke first in America?

ELTON: Well, it had come out in England and died. It had come out in May of 1970, got into the BBC chart at 45, and went straight out again. (The BBC LP chart contains 50 albums.) We thought it would get into the charts cuz it was a special type album with orchestra and all kinds of things. We had a crisis meeting to say "why isn't it on the charts?" "why isn't it selling?" and I didn't want to go on the road, I just didn't want to know. They said, "you're just going to have to go out on the road and promote it." So I thought, all right, I'm gonna have to. We went to the States primarily because the record company said "you come over here, we'll break this". I didn't believe them, I really went to the States to have a look at some record stores. And also it was either join Jeff Beck or go to the States, or Jeff Beck was going to join us, but it turned out we would have had to join Jeff Beck, it was one of those ego things. So we went to the States and it broke. I wasn't surprised because there was so much hype going on I could have believed anything that was going on when I was over there. I would have believed it if the record had gone straight in at number one. There was so much, my head was going round and round and round. It was a totally different thing to what had happened over in England. It did eventually get in the charts, although it didn't get in while we were over there. It started to climb when we went back for the seven-week tour at the end of the year, after doing the "Friends" soundtrack. When it was 17 with a bullet in *Cashbox* and we were one above Graham Nash or David Crosby or somebody like that it was so immense I couldn't believe it, I was so knocked out. We were so surprised it was happening in America because it had been out in England and hadn't done a bloody thing. If it hadn't have broken in America it would have just died a death.

BERNIE: It's strange, because I don't remember anything about that period of time. I can't remember dates.

ELTON: I always say it was 1971 I happened, but it was 1970.

BERNIE: It was all just one night, that one night at the Troubadour.

ELTON: It really was just that first night, like you said, like "The Eddy Duchin Story" or "dis boy is a genius". One of those old films, "look, the boy is conducting the orchestra he's 14 years old and he's blind and he's got one leg and everybody's going 'hooray!'"

BERNIE: The next morning, like, wham, bam, there on

the front of all the papers . . . it's just . . . (sighs).

ELTON: People were flocking to us. I couldn't believe it. Second night I played Leon Russell was in the front row but I didn't see him until the last number. Thank God I didn't, because at that time I slept and drunk Leon Russell. I mean I still really like him, but at that time I regarded him as some kind of god. And I saw him and I just stopped. He said, "keep on", and he shouted something, and I said, oh fuck, and he said "come up to the house tomorrow", and I figured, this was it, he's going to tie me up in a chair and whip me and say "listen here, you bastard, *this* is how you play the piano" but he was really nice instead. It was like schoolboy's fantasies coming true. Really strange. Quincy Jones . . .

BERNIE: All the pop stars . . .

ELTON: Quincy Jones, he must have brought his whole family, he has 900 children, Quincy Jones, and I kept shaking hands coming through the door. The whole week at the Troubadour should have been called The Million Handshakes. That's all I did. I couldn't tell you who I met. So many people wanted to meet me. I just stood there and [publicist] Norman Winter was saying "this is a very heavy cat, from the *Detroit Evening Puddle*, and he's flown out to see you" and I would say "oh, really nice to meet you." Looking back I did so many outrageous things on that tour. David Ackles was on the bill. I mean, *that* was the first thing I couldn't believe, that we were playing *above* David Ackles. In England he had much more prestige than he apparently had in America, he apparently hadn't been working much that year, and I said "what about people like Tom Paxton and Tim Buckley?" and they'd say "oh no, they very rarely work" and I'd feel that was really strange. We couldn't believe we were playing above David Ackles.

BERNIE: It freaked us out to find out he was even on the bill, because we didn't find out until we went there in the afternoon, did we?

ELTON: We thought, well, obviously David Ackles is top of the bill. It was just weird, all these fantasies . . . and the record company would come down in the afternoon and say "gee, fellas, it's all gonna happen tonight, it's gonna be a mind-fucker," and we were saying "who are all these people?" It was very, very weird. I loved it, though. I went to Disneyland and sang "Your Song" on stage in shorts and Mickey Mouse ears. Looking back on it I think it's horrific. I mean, when we went back the second time and I was big enough to play Santa Monica Civic on my own for one night and Ry Cooder was first on the bill and then Odetta and then us. I had four suits of clothing on. I had this cape on, and this hat, you know where in the *Don't Shoot Me* book where I've got the top hat and the cape, that was the night in Santa Monica. I took that off and had a jump suit on. Took that off and I had another sort of jump suit on. Then I took that off and had a long Fillmore West sweater. Maxine had gone out and said (imitating Maxine)

23

"Ooh, I've found these mauve tights, I bet you wouldn't wear them on stage", and I said I would, and this was all filmed, it was on the Henry Mancini show. [Bernie in hysterics.] Oh weird!

ELTON: I mean, I look back and say, fuck me, did they actually happen, all those things?

SONGS

PG: Of course one thing that had to do with the initial American success was "Your Song".

ELTON: No, the album began to move before they took the single off. "Border Song" had come out and been covered by a lot of people, Dorothy Morrison crept into the chart and we crept into the chart, but the album started to move . . . well, the album coincided with the single going up . . . yeah, the single did help, you're right, it helped a lot. And then it was released over here as a result and became a hit.

PG: You're still fond of that song. You still do it.

ELTON: Yeah, well, I think when people think of Elton John they think of either "Your Song" or "Crocodile Rock". You know what I mean? I don't get fed up with singing it at all. I really liked the Billy Paul version of it.

PG: What about the Andy Williams version?

ELTON: Well, the Andy Williams version is the stock Andy Williams version. He can't really do much else, can he?

PG: John Walters [a BBC producer] said he went up to you at your wedding and said "If I were a bridegroom, but then again, no"——

BERNIE: He always says that. (Laughter.) He's always got a different line, he comes up to me and says things like, "If I were a disc jockey, but then again, no". They're always different.

PG: Did you ever think that line was, I think what he was trying to say, a cop-out?

BERNIE: I never thought it was anything. I mean, no.

ELTON: That song is so old.

BERNIE: I can't even remember writing that song.

ELTON: I remember the girl you were going out with, the girl you wrote it about.

BERNIE: I didn't write it about anybody.

ELTON: I thought you wrote . . .

BERNIE: Well, that wasn't . . .

ELTON: Still, you were quite steep. When you did have your little affairs and things you got very steeped in them.

BERNIE: Yes, but I never aimed that song at anybody.

ELTON: But "First Episode at Heinton" was——

BERNIE: Oh, yes, that was. I forgot about that. See, I forget about songs, I have to be reminded.

ELTON: Somebody says to me, play the songs off *Tumbleweed*, I can't even remember the songs on the album.

BERNIE: The biggest confidence trick as far as a song is concerned to me is "Take Me to the Pilot". It's so great that so many people have covered that and sort of put their all into it and that song means fuck-all, it doesn't mean *anything*.

ELTON: We're doing a documentary, and I said it's

probably the most unlikely song of all-time to be covered, because of the words.

BERNIE: They don't mean anything.

ELTON: It's had so many covers, Ben E. King . . .

BERNIE: That song proves what you can get away with.

ELTON: It's like Marc [Bolan], really. You can string a lot of words together that sound good together that don't mean anything, like "I Am the Walrus".

PG: Has anybody ever asked you about any religious insights?

ELTON: Oh, I was just going to say that.

BERNIE: That was a great one.

ELTON: People thought we were anti-Semitic, we were everything . . .

BERNIE: Do you remember "I Need You to Turn To?" The guy who came in, that college guy, and thought it was about the crucifiction? We said "how on earth can you say it's about the crucifiction?" and he proceeded to condense it and to change all the meanings. One line was great. He said about being "nailed to your love in many lonely nights", thinking that being "nailed to your love" was being nailed to the cross. That's amazing. That's like "Puff, the Magic Dragon". "Puff, the Magic Drag-on" . . .

ELTON: Puff was really a transvestite. (Laughter.) You always find people who are willing to read things into songs. They're the sort of people who write in to the back page of *Melody Maker*. They're idiots, I mean, how can you possibly write to the back page of

27

Melody Maker? You'd have to be a bit demented. "I think Eric Clapton is God and I think Black Sabbath are rubbish. So there! Stick that in your pipe and smoke it!" (Bernie is convulsed at Elton's impersonation of a female pop fan.) It's so fucking stupid. Like there's a letter this week "Bernie Taupin and Elton John have too much focus on his image". It's very interesting. "He's gone with the thoughtful songs like 'Country Comfort'." I mean, "Country Comfort", a thoughtful song? "And on his new album he's cast all of these aside." I would say "Daniel" and "Have Mercy on the Criminal" are far more thoughtful than "Country Comfort". I mean, that's a song that really did drive us mad. We had to stop singing that one.

BERNIE: I think the band were going to lynch him if he didn't stop singing it.

ELTON: You really do get people who get pissed off because you don't play it. We get shouts for the most obscure things. "Burn Down the Mission," we haven't done that on stage for two years, and they still shout out for that.

BERNIE: "Burn Down the Mission" became our national anthem, our "Street Fighting Man". People came to expect it and it became so sort of plastic at the end that I'd stand behind the curtain and go da-da-da-da-da-kick away the stool, right——

ELTON: I just couldn't stand it any more.

BERNIE: It became so mechanical.

ELTON: That was about the end of 1971, when the

band were really getting pissed off and I was really getting pissed off because we'd done all we could really do as a three-piece unit. Piano, bass, and drums, I mean it wasn't even *organ*, bass and drums. Very odd, piano, bass, and drums. I don't know how we ever made out, really, because it's like a very heavy Ramsey Lewis Trio. Don't know how I did it, it's bad enough now. We were so bored we didn't even look forward to playing any more.

BERNIE: We were really surprised with the new guitarist because we were scared of it being overpowering with mountains of amplifiers and microphones.

ELTON: I'd seen Davey, he played on the *Madman* session, he was with a folk group called Magna Carta, and I just happened to mention to Gus that I'd give anything to have someone like him in the band. I think Gus mentioned it to Davey and Davey said I'd love to join. I mean, I never ever met Dave. The first time I ever met Davey was in France, as far as talking about the band goes. We never really met him until we went to make *Honky Chateau*. And it's just made the whole difference, you know. A much happier thing, and it's much easier to play with four people. Most three-piece groups wind up breaking up.

PG: You talked about "First Episode" actually meaning something. What was that?

BERNIE: Well, it means what it says, we were just saying that it *was* directed at somebody. It was directed at somebody I was at school with. I mean, the story's the story, and that's as far as it goes, really. I never thought "oh, that's a good one, I'll sit down and write", it was another case of me starting a song and the idea coming along as I was writing it. It was just about a schoolboy crush, really. That's a very old song, really. [Copyright 1968.]

ELTON: That's really a poem, it wasn't really a lyric, was it?

BERNIE: Yeah, see, trying to remember how I constructed those songs is very difficult because it's such a long time ago, I can't remember the background behind them, I just know I did them, and they are what they are.

PG: You mention the difference between poems and lyrics. What you did on your first album you'd call poems.

BERNIE: On my album, yeah. I'm always trying to put that across, there's such a great difference between writing poetry and writing lyrics for rock and roll, and I really sort of get annoyed when people class my lyrics as poetry, because they certainly aren't. If my lyrics were put in a book and put out as a poetry book, if people thought that was good poetry ... hmmm ... well, more power to them ... hmmm ... I'm sorry, there's two different fields, really, and you can't bridge the gap. One is one and the other is the other.

ELTON: What about "Daniel", who is obviously a homosexual? Somebody said it's obviously a homosexual song, Daniel, my brother, I love you——

BERNIE: Who said that?

ELTON: Some skinhead in Manchester. He said "that 'Crocodile Rock' is rubbish, and 'Daniel' is a homosexual song, isn't it?"

BERNIE: No! Did he? A lot of people have thought I was writing about my brother, because I do have a brother in Spain. But Daniel in the song is a one-eyed war veteran who is just saying 'the only place I can live in peace is in Spain'.

ELTON: So many people have said they can't understand what 'Daniel' means. It's because I left the last verse out. I still think it's quite self-explanatory.

BERNIE: People got their knickers completely in a twist just because Levon called his son Jesus and he was a balloon salesman. Just because he didn't call his child "George", and he wasn't a mechanic or something. I don't know, the story's completely simple, it's just about a guy who wants to get away from his father's hold over him. Strange.

ELTON: Then there was the whole Jewish thing.

BERNIE: Oh, the anti-Semitic period, where everybody thought "Border Song" was anti-Semitic. Don't ask me why, I don't know. Most of my friends are Jewish. I married one. (Laughter.)

ELTON: Going back to "Border Song", it's never been disclosed, but I wrote the lyrics for the last verse, because it was only two verses long and we thought it really needed another one. That's why the last verse is very mundane. That's never been disclosed before . . .

PG: Is that the only verse of a song you've written?

ELTON: Oh, yes.

PG: A lot of the critics, especially in America, have had fun trying to identify the songs that influenced you for "Crocodile Rock".

ELTON: Oh, I've always wanted to write a song——

BERNIE: We got sued by the people who wrote "Speedy Gonzales".

ELTON: Yeah, but they dropped that. I mean, that's so stupid. But there are the obvious ones, "Oh, Carol"—we wrote one song, "Rock and Roll Madonna", I always wanted to write one song, a nostalgic song, a rock and roll song which captured the right sounds. "Crocodile Rock" is just a combination of so many songs, really. "Little Darling", "Oh, Carol", some Beach Boys influences, they're in there as well, I suppose. Eddie Cochran. I mean, it's just a combination of songs. People say it's like Freddie Cannon. We've written a new one, "Your Mama Can't Twist", and everyone's gonna go, "you've pinched it from Loggins and Messina!"

BERNIE: Loggins and Messina? *What*?

ELTON: "Your Mama Don't Dance." Oh, well. It all comes from the sub-conscious. There's Del Shannon in there, that high stuff. And I love Bobby Vee. He was so much to me. There was this big party in California, all the biggies were invited, and there I was in the corner talking to Bobby Vee . . . I've just started "You Mama Can't Twist".

BERNIE: What does it sound like?

ELTON: Well, the beginning is like the Beatles' "Twist and Shout". Just the beginning, don't worry. It's not an actual nick, it's just got the same tempo. Then we'll have on the next album a song with the feel of "Palisades Park". I used to love Freddie Cannon. I hear he's a promotion man at Warner Brothers now. You deserve a tribute, Freddie.

PG: Elton mentioned a little Beach Boys influence on "Crocodile Rock". Backstage the other night you told me Brian Wilson influenced "Rocket Man".

BERNIE: What I meant was, and I don't know why, I had the same idea for it as "A Day in the Life of a Tree", the same feeling, that sort of spacey feeling. When I wrote "Rocket Man" I thought that was a good idea, not that in any way I wanted them to *sound* the same.

PG: Elton said at one point that "Teenage Idol" was written with thoughts of Marc. Is that true?

BERNIE: As far as I'm concerned it wasn't written exactly *about* Marc. He was the sort of image I was talking about, and it just so happens that he was the closest person to associate with that song. So we just sort of dedicate it to him in our own minds.

PG: You've said you generally start with a first line or two and grow from there. Do you do this mostly at home and do you use a musical instrument?

BERNIE: It varies. I could never define to anybody the way I write a song, because it varies so much. Sometimes I'll just come up with a title and I'll try to write a song around that title. Other times I'll come up with a first line or a first two lines. With "Rocket Man" the first two lines came to me when I was driving along. I just thought...hmmm, can't remember what the first two lines are...hmmm... well, whatever they were, they came to me as I was driving along and by the time I'd gotten home I'd written the song in my head. I got inside and had to rush and write it all down before I'd forgotten it. Seldom do I think I'd like to write a song about a particular subject or person, and sit down from scratch. Usually it's either a first line, a line somewhere in it, or a title, then the song comes alive.

Basically it takes me very little time to write a song. If I find myself taking more than an hour to do it I usually forget it, and try something else. I like to work quickly, I never like to waste any time. I never write half of a song and come back to it later at all. It all has to be done at once. I lose interest if it doesn't.

PG: I understand when you came back from Jamaica you came back with a load of songs.

BERNIE: Actually I didn't write anything in Jamaica, I'd written them all before we went there. He wrote the majority of the songs over there. I wrote all my parts about a month before. He just took them with him. I got about twenty songs done in possibly two weeks. I really got down to it and it came across quickly. I felt very prolific at that time, I guess.

PG: The next album won't be recorded until May. Are you worried about accumulating a back-log, or imposing on yourself a period where you won't write songs?

BERNIE: We're going to be recording in May, and I've

34

only heard the songs in their finished state once, so I'm not bored of them. I want to hear them again, but I'm holding myself back so I don't hear them again until they're recorded. Once they're recorded I won't hear them until the finished mix, so they'll still be fresh songs to me. Once it's released it'll be like a new album for me and I won't have to start working on the next one until six months or so after that.

PG: So you'll have plenty of time for your other projects.

BERNIE: Sure. Like I said, it took two weeks to write twenty songs, and I only have to write two albums worth a year, so that's on the whole about twenty-four songs. It takes me a month to write twenty-four songs.

PG: The only songs I've heard from the new album, quite obviously, are the two Elton has done on stage. There has been talk of a third title, "Jamaican Jerk-Off". Is that for real?

BERNIE: We're changing that now because people would probably take that the wrong way and think we're having a go at Jamaica. We originally wanted to write something like "Jamaica Twist", but it turned out to be a calypso-type "Jamaican Jerk-Off". I think now we've decided to call it "Jamaica Jerk". Have we?

ELTON: I don't know yet.

BERNIE: It's not rude or anything. Well, it's not very rude.

PG: I just asked Bernie if the new album was going to be greatly different.

ELTON: Well, to start with, it's going to be two albums released simultaneously, or a double album, whichever works out. We've got enough songs to put out. It's going to be far more musical, nothing like *Don't Shoot Me*. There will still be rock-and-roll songs——

BERNIE: I don't think we'll be able to tell until it's done!

ELTON: I've got a vision in my mind as to how I want it to sound, though.

BERNIE: I've never been so excited about a bunch of songs before.

ELTON: It's a great feeling to get twenty-five songs done.

BERNIE: Twenty-five? It's gone up now?

ELTON: Twenty-two. It will be twenty-five by the time you write *some more* (firmly).

BERNIE: Well, we've only got twenty now——

ELTON: But you're going to write more anyhow, aren't you?

BERNIE: I might.

ELTON AND BERNIE AT THE MOVIES

PG: How did you get involved with "Friends"?

ELTON: It was a time——

BERNIE: I don't remember how it started——

ELTON: I remember. It was a time, it was the year we broke in the States, 1970. It was early on in the year and we were pretty cold everywhere and nothing really was happening and John Gilbert, whose father was making the film, approached us after hearing the *Elton John* album. They approached us and we agreed to do it, agreed to a sum of money they would pay us in advance.

BERNIE: It was all done in a very straightforward fashion and in fact I was the first one to get the script——

ELTON: You wrote one of the songs before you ever saw the script! "Michelle's Song."

BERNIE: Yeah, well, I guess we thought it was quite neat to do a film score. I just read the script and half-way through the script I wrote one song and then by the time I'd finished the script the three songs that were actually written for the film were done and the other songs were things we'd just had hanging about, and they stuck them into the film.

ELTON: Well, we didn't spend any time doing it. We'd gotten back from the States the first time and then because we'd had success there we had to go back to the States four weeks later for this sort of first major tour. All the "Friends" stuff had to be done in four weeks, it was such a panic session. So it was really a drama. Plus they wanted to release a soundtrack album, and I didn't want them to release a soundtrack album with three songs on it and fill it out with garbage, motorists peeing by lakes and things like that, so we said, well, we got two spare songs, have those, "Honeyroll" and "Can I Put You On", which we'd been doing on stage anyway, so they put them on during transistor radio sequences. We put them on the album as a bonus, really. I really regret that because, fuck, I would have wanted to put them on our own album.

BERNIE: Music people and record people really don't hit it off——

ELTON: You mean film people.

BERNIE: What did I say?

ELTON: You said music people and record people.

BERNIE: Sorry. Record people and film people. Like when we first cut the original soundtrack we did at Olympic we had all these people coming in, film people whom we didn't know, trying to command the session, saying you should do this and you shouldn't do that. That's why we went and re-did it at Trident because we didn't have them around.

ELTON: You really need a steely mind like John Barry

to do it. He's got it down to a fine art. I couldn't do it. It was like working in a bank or working at a computer. You have to write forty seconds of music and if you don't write forty seconds it's a disaster. I'd never ever do it again.

PG: You said in the car the sales on that were sort of hyped up.

ELTON: I think so. It was the only album we've ever had——

BERNIE: Why, with that beautiful cover they had on it.

ELTON: Oh, this is a great story. Paramount will love this. We were proud of what we had done. We wouldn't have let it go out otherwise. I thought it was a pretty good soundtrack. We said, alright, all our albums have had pretty good covers, let us do the packaging. We sent the guy at Paramount a *Tumbleweed* album and said we thought it was a pretty good package and he said no, it's rubbish, we'll come up with something better. There you go. Their "better thing" was that fucking pink massacre. The album came out in the States, Paramount rushed it out because we were riding on the crest of a wind, with two albums in the charts, and they released it and it was the first album we'd ever had that was gold on the day of issue. I couldn't believe it. Of course, I was pretty naive in those days, and believed it. (Elton's mother's biscuits are passed around.) Munch, munch, munch, the sound of biscuits . . . All those albums came back, I'm sure. You can go into any record store in the States now and see *Friends* for $1.98 with a hole punched through. I mean, it was definitely one of the first bootleg gold albums. I think a few people at Paramount lost their jobs over that. It was just amazing, wasn't it?

BERNIE: I just couldn't face . . . I wouldn't mind writing a song for a film or a few songs for a film as long as I didn't have to put up with all that shit that gets laid down at times.

ELTON: It was just like "Midnight Cowboy", using that already recorded thing.

BERNIE: Yeah, right. If somebody came to me and said, come and see this film, and it was a good film that was worthwhile, and I could just write a song for it, I think I'd do it.

ELTON: I think incidental music in films is boring anyway. It really is, in the classic [sings "Dragnet" theme] sense. But I mean things like "Easy Rider" have music in them which has already been recorded. It can be just as effective. It's all bullshit, that you *must* write such-and-such. I mean, most film music is so dreadful.

BERNIE: I got a thing yesterday asking me if I wrote "Everybody's Talking".

ELTON: Really?

BERNIE: Yeah.

ELTON: You should have wrote back saying yes, we did. Fred Neil probably wouldn't like that very much . . .

PG: Elton has never seen the film in a cinema,

although he has seen some of the rushes. Have you ever seen it?

BERNIE: No. (Laughter.) I never want to, either!

ELTON: It's very hard to find a cinema where it was playing, actually.

BERNIE: I think the film did a record run of two days in the West End, didn't it?

ELTON: All our relations went to see it. My aunt said, "Oh, I loved it, I thought the film was lovely, chasing through the woods with all that lovely music going on." It will probably do very well in Japan. Bloody nips ... (Laughter from Bernie.) It was just a thing that came out at the wrong time. As far as I can tell the music was bloody sensational, compared to what the film was. In all fairness, the people who made the film were fantastic for us. I just said, you have to write forty seconds of film music but Paul Buckmaster had written forty seconds of our theme and it turned out forty-seven and they said, well, that's alright, we'll extend the car chase by seven seconds. They were really nice people, I'm not putting them down at all, in fact they gave us so much freedom, but even so ...

BERNIE: It was the bigwigs who fucked it all up.

ELTON: They're the ones who took hold of it and destroyed it. Imagine if we'd had someone really strict, we'd have been around the bend.

BERNIE: I don't think it would have ever come out.

ELTON: It would never have seen the light of day. Film people are so fucking arrogant. I hate them. I saw Sam Peckinpagh, we went to the set of one of his films, and oh dear, oh dear, I would have liked to have smashed him right in the fucking mouth. He said, "oh, I must lie down, you did that take wrong." I know it's artistic temperment, but really. I wouldn't mind if he had ever made a decent movie.

PG: Why did you do "Born to Boogie"?

ELTON: Well, I mean, why did I do my three minutes? Marc said, "could you just come down and we're gonna just do 'Tutti Frutti' and a couple of things, it'll be fun." It was nice, I met Ringo. I had never met Ringo before. I didn't know I was going to be in it that much. It was a nice thing to play. A lot of the music you heard on there ... the "Children of the Revolution" we recorded at that session was so much better than Marc's single. It only took four hours, it was nice to do. Ringo was nice. All we really did was play for four hours, we didn't pose or anything. They must have lots of stuff they didn't use. Like I've said before, in that I look like a fucking gorilla, so ugly.

PG: What about the Bryan Forbes documentary, how's that coming along?

ELTON: Bryan has wanted to do something for a long time. It's going to be sort of a process, he shows Bernie writing a song, me writing the music, recording it, and playing it on stage. It's *not* going to be boring. I mean, it's very tongue-in-cheek, he's shot me in the bath. [Shows pictures.]

BERNIE: Hey, Elton, you got a hairy bum!

PG: So the film has no similarity to "Born to Boogie"?

42

ELTON: Oh, no, there's hardly any music at all. Some people still think you just walk into a recording studio, sit around a microphone, and that's it. This is just showing what happens, and tries to show a different side of me. The back side. Tata!

PG: When will it be ready?

ELTON: Exactly the same time as the album, so it'll be pre-sold around the world. It's not going to be like "Mad Dogs and Englishmen". I can't stand all those films. "Woodstock" was the one good one, and that was it. They're so boring. I came out of "Mad Dogs and Englishmen" and felt I'd done an American tour.

BERNIE: Two and a half hours we had to sit there, it made me feel so dirty, it was so grotty . . .

ELTON: Everybody looked like they needed a good wash. The only good thing about it was Claudia Linnear wobbling her tits around, that was the only stimulating thing. And Leon, his piano playing.

PG: So you really don't have much to do with the content of the Forbes film.

ELTON: Oh no, I don't know what Bernie's gonna say and Bernie doesn't know what I'm gonna say.

GIGS WE HAVE KNOWN

PG: How did the live album come about?

ELTON: We had this guy who worked for WABC and he is an Elton John freak, or at least was, probably not now, I didn't send him a Christmas card. He was always trying to badger us into doing this concert because he wanted to inaugurate live concerts on the air in New York, in the studio. The first time we said no and the second time they came back to us and said we'll put you into a recording studio instead of a WABC studio so we said yes, alright. So they got . . . what was the name of the place?

BERNIE: A & R Studios.

ELTON: On 7th Avenue. So we just did it one evening with a hundred people in there and it went out live on the air. I didn't know at the time that it was going on eight-track. As far as I was concerned it was just going out over the airwaves of New York.

BERNIE: Oh, we had no intention at that time of recording it for an album.

ELTON: I'm very anti-live album, as a matter of fact. Well, we recorded it and listened to it back, on the eight-track. It was a time when people were coming to see me and people were buying my records and the two of them weren't getting together. Everybody thought I was going to be a very moody person on stage, fainting after every three songs. And I thought the band weren't getting any credit, Nigel and Dee, and that it would be nice to do the album as sort of a bootleg cover, that Nigel and Dee would be able to earn some money out of it. Of course, if you do it live over the air in America and thousands of people are at home with their stereo equipment, you're gonna get stereo tape recording and bootlegging. I think genuinely we lost 100,000 sales from bootlegs.

BERNIE: It was such a good thing to bootleg, it was right there in stereo for them. If they had good equipment, plug it into the radio and there you have it.

ELTON: I think it's a fucking good live album in that most live albums are the result of say, six days' recording. If you're gonna make a live recording you get a truck to come down to two or three performances and you choose the best ones so it really isn't a live album. It's like doing a session album, which take is the best over three nights? Ours was just totally live, we didn't know anything about it.

BERNIE: The American pressing was much, much better than the English pressing.

ELTON: The American mix was mixed at Trident and the British mix was mixed at DJM Studios. It's just totally mind-blowing. The English mix is very dull and dreary, the American record is very good. [During the conversation Elton has been examining the cover of *Rolling Stone* #84, which showed him in boots.

Finally he breaks out laughing.]

ELTON: I used to think those were really high heels. I thought those boots were really hip because they had high heels. Shit!

BERNIE: I remember when you got those. They were so outrageous because they had stars on them and they were silver.

PG: Now you say you won't wear anything except the heels you're wearing now.

ELTON: I feel so short, I never wear really short shoes. I rarely wear tennis shoes. I'm 5'8", I hate being short. I'm sure I *will* wear something that's flatter. I mean, in a couple of years time I'll probably look at a picture of me in platforms and say "what the hell was I doing?" Those are, again, disposable. Everything's becoming disposable. Disposable me, disposable . . . (makes shrivelling up noise).

PG: On this tour, that is, the English tour, you've been more seemingly low-keyed in the presentation of the show than in the American tours.

ELTON: The leaping about?

PG: And the special effects.

ELTON: Right, the special effects thing, we thought about doing it, but we thought let's just get this tour over and done with, because we never look forward to touring England right after America because it's sort of an anti-climax. This time it hasn't been, though I don't leap about much now, only towards the end of the show. I'd just rather sit there and concentrate. It's a bit obvious. There's only so much

Elton John

Bernie Taupin

Elton at the time of the release of "Border Song" on Primrose Hill

Bernie and Norma Jean and Elton at home.

*Elton and Rod Stewart in training
at Watford Football Club*

On stage at the Crystal Palace
Garden Party.

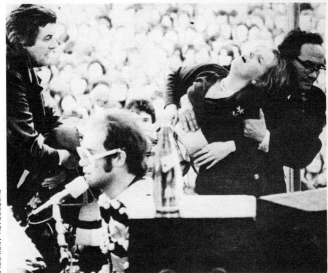

In concert at Watford Football Ground,
May 1974.

Elton photographed for the release of 'Tumbleweed Connection'...

leaping about that can be done, and that's it. I really enjoy it, but, for example, we don't do "Madman Across the Water" on stage because it's too drawn out. With an American audience you can draw it out and draw it out, but with an English audience you have to hold their attention all the time. With America they don't mind what you do with them, in England they really manipulate you. You can't afford to do four slow numbers together, otherwise they get really pissed off, whereas in America you can. But we're still on stage for 1¾ hours, I think.

PG: What have you got ready for the next American tour, or have you started thinking about that yet?

ELTON: We have. I'm not going to do a lengthy American tour, as far as ten weeks goes or anything like that, I think the days of doing those are over. It kills you, it just physically kills you. I've got a couple of ideas, I think a couple of dates on the next American are going to be very bizarre. Not bizarre weirdo, like the Cockettes or anything, but bizarre show-biz. We got a nice idea for the Hollywood Bowl if we get the date.

BERNIE: We're gonna blow the audience up.

ELTON: Steinway have offered to build me a special piano. I would like to get a special piano made, and as far as visuals go, I think visuals are very important to me, not in the sense of an act like Alice Cooper who's got it down to a fine art, but in the sense of high camp and just very, very tongue-in-cheek. We did "Singing in the Rain" as a tongue-in-cheek thing on

47

the last American tour, "Legs" Larry Smith and I, it was his suggestion, and I said "you must be mad, they'll wonder what the fuck's going on," but they loved it! They'd sing along with it and I thought well, there you go. The act is going to become a little more Liberaceized, not in a clothes sense, or Busby Berkeleyized, I'd like to have nine pianos on stage, a cascade of pianos, and make my entrance like that. Just give the audience a really nice sort of show. I don't like to look at groups who come out looking like they've just been drowned for five years at Big Sur. A lot of English people are very theatrical, like the Faces for example, and I think that's why the American kids like it. I could never go on stage in denims.

PG: Of the pianists, you've mentioned Liberace, and many people have said there's a lot of Jerry Lee Lewis influence in your jumping about, but you said in the car you're not really a big Lewis admirer.

ELTON: Well, I used to be until I saw him, and then I went off him a bit. I still think his rock and roll records are amazing, but I'm more a Little Richard stylist than a Jerry Lee Lewis, I think. Jerry Lee is a very intricate piano player and very skilful, whereas I think Little Richard was more of a pounder. I think his rock and roll records were the best rock and roll records ever made, as far as just the genuine sound on them goes. Apart from "Hound Dog", which is amazing.

BERNIE: The stuff Jerry Lee Lewis is into at the moment——

ELTON: It's just taking the country road, which so many people do, and he treats his audience like shit, which I've never ever done.

BERNIE: He treats everybody like that, smoking his big fucking cigars, and pretending he's such a heavy.

ELTON: And calling himself "The Killer". I could kill more people with one finger than he did when I saw him. I always find rock and roll acts like that now pathetic. I mean, I've seen them all, and I feel it's sad ... Someone said the other day "Neil Sedaka is growing old gracefully", you know what I mean, he's still making good music and he's not having to go up there in a leather suit and sing "Oh Carol". Everybody I've seen like Little Richard, Jerry Lee Lewis, Chuck Berry and all those sort of people, I'm afraid, are extremely pathetic. I feel sad. Chuck Berry is God, but what has he written for ... I mean, people say he wrote all those great rock and roll songs and we never wrote any, but at least we're still writing things. He hasn't written anything decent for fifteen years. It amazes me why everybody exults him. Why, Muddy Waters can grow old gracefully, you can still go see Muddy Waters and enjoy him. He'll still play "Got My Mojo Working", but he'll throw something new in. I think it's about time all this Chuck Berry idolizing came to a halt. I can dig the nostalgia trip, and I dig his old records, but I find that side of the business very irritating. I feel sorry for them. I wouldn't like in fifteen years time to still be playing "Crocodile Rock". I think for the life span he's lasted, Chuck Berry's productivity has been nil, more or less.

PG: Bernie, you were going to say something about Jerry Lee's album.

BERNIE: *The Session* album, I mean there's so much shit going on about that. I'ts such a nothing album, there's no fire in it whatsoever, it's plastic.

ELTON: It's like those Little Richard Reprise albums, they're all so diabolical.

BERNIE: Who wants to hear Jerry Lee Lewis doing "Proud Mary" and saying "The Killer's gonna get ya." I mean, every track he throws in these little asides, like "Pff, pff, I'm the Killer," you know. It's, yecch, it's sick, I can't stand all that. There's this big fuss about all his heavy friends on the album, there's hardly anybody on that album of any great note.

ELTON: Well, Peter Frampton and Al Lee. It's just that Mercury Records decided to have this great hype and invited everybody who was anybody. I mean, they invited me to play on it, which was ludicrous. What am I supposed to do, play piano for Jerry Lee Lewis, I mean the guy's technically brilliant enough to eat me for breakfast. It's just that he's so lazy he won't do it. And Rod Stewart. What's Rod gonna do on it, sing for him? It should have been called *"Jerry Lewis' Session*, starring Rod Stewart, who sings for Jerry Lee, and Elton John, who plays for Jerry Lee. Jerry was in Nashville when this album was recorded, *but*, his spirit was there."

50

BERNIE: Don't read this, Jerry, don't read this!

PG: Are you often asked to play with other people?

ELTON: I always used to be, but I think there are probably better session pianists around than me. My name is valuable, but there's always Billy Preston, and if I was Ringo Starr I'd rather have Billy Preston playing on his record than me. I'd rather have Nicky Hopkins, probably, because they're so good. They can fit in so easily. I'm always willing to play if I'm interested, but I don't get offered much. I don't think I'm that much respected as a pianist. I used to a lot of sessions, I used to play on the Hollies records. "He Ain't Heavy, He's My Brother," and all that. I used to do far more sessions than I do now.

PG: What are some of the records you're on?

ELTON: I used to make records, you know those cheap versions of hits? I used to do back-up vocals for those, and then I did Stevie Wonder's "Signed, Sealed, Delivered", a cover of "United We Stand", "My Baby Loves Loving", and I used to do the "ooh"s and "ahh"s. The lead singer of Uriah Heep, David Byron, used to sing all the lead vocals. There was a record over here, you probably never heard it, called "Back Home" by the World Cup Football Squad, and try to record that, we used to stand there and laugh. The guy who did it still does them, I think, he used to be with the Tornadoes. We used to do it, go around to the pub, have a few drinks, come back, and just collapse. Musically, they were very good, the best cover versions of any of those sort. Donna

Gillespie used to do them, she's in "Superstar". It was great fun singing somebody else's songs. I mean, some of those things, the songs were so awful, "I'll be your jack-in-the-box", and we used to go "whoop-doop-doop".

BERNIE: And Robin Gibb!

ELTON: Oh, I did a cover version for a Dutch record company once of "Saved By the Bell", and I *literally* did it like that. (Sings his Robin Gibb impersonation.) They did five takes of that and by the end m/ neck was really red, sort of hanging down there like a chicken. So I've done all that, I can't remember it all. My whole week used to be taken up by session work. I did the Scaffold sessions as well. Doing their sessions was another laugh, I mean, you just couldn't stop laughing, they were so funny. They used to take hours. The Barron Knights—all the funny people.

BERNIE: I remember the Barron Knights session.

ELTON: That was when the Beatles had "Hey Jude" out because Paul McCartney brought a copy into the studio and played it for them. They used to make records like "Here Come the Olympic Games", and change words.

BERNIE: They were really great.

ELTON: They were really funny. I never did a session I thought was a real drag. (Bernie starts singing the "Olympic Games" song.)

LIFE IN BRITAIN

PG: One report in the national press awhile back said you'd once almost gotten married to a millionairess.

ELTON: Me?

PG: And called it off three weeks before?

ELTON: Oh, that's true. I wouldn't say she was a millionairess, that's the national press boosting their headlines, "One-Armed Man Swims Channel" or something like that, you know what I mean. It was a girl I met when I was in Sheffield that miserable Christmas doing cabaret with John Baldry. She was six foot tall and going out with a midget in Sheffield who drove around in a Mini with special pedals on. He used to beat her up! I felt so sorry for her and she followed me up the next week to South Shields—this gets even more romantic, folks—and I fell desperately in love and said come down to London and we'll find a flat. Eventually we got a nice flat in this dismal area. It was a very stormy six months, after which I was on the verge of a nervous breakdown. I attempted to commit suicide and various other things, during which Bernie and I wrote nil, absolutely nothing.

BERNIE: Don't forget the gas.

ELTON: I tried to commit suicide one day. It was a very Woody Allen type suicide. I turned on the gas and left all the windows open. (Laughter.)

BERNIE: I remember when I told Linda and said, my God, he's tried to commit suicide, and she said, why, he's wasted all the gas!

ELTON: It was just like six months of hell. I got the flat, I bought all the furniture, the cake was made, it was three weeks away, Baldry was going to be best man, and in the end Baldry, we were out in the Speakeasy ... no, it was the Bag of Nails ... no ...

BERNIE: It was the Bag of Nails.

ELTON: Baldry was there, and one of the Supremes— one of the Supremes used to go out with the singer of Bluesology, how about *that* for a piece of gossip— Cindy Birdsong used to go out with our singer. Anyway, we're there at the Bag of Nails and Baldry is saying "you're mad, man, you're mad, you don't love her," and I was saying "I do, I do," and he was saying "she beats you up, she smashes you on the face," and we got more and more depressed sitting there until four in the morning, setting off burglar alarms when we staggered out and I shouted "It's over, it's finished!" and then came a couple of days of hell. In the end my Dad came with his Ford Cortina and how he managed to cram all that stuff in there I don't know and my mother said "If you marry her I'll never speak to you again"—oh, it was just amazing. So she sued me for breach of promise and all that shit. She got away with quite a lot of money in shares.

BERNIE: It was so outrageous . . .

ELTON: It was outrageous because she was six foot and she used to beat me up and *she* used to be beaten up by a midget, so how about that? It was so weird. You know, I have always expected her to show up one of these days.

PG: John Baldry you did the album for with Rod.

ELTON: Right, we did two albums, half each, so I see John quite a lot.

PG: Will you keep doing that?

ELTON: I don't think so. I don't think it's good for John. The first album was a good idea, it got up to seventy-something in *Billboard*, sold quite well and he went over and toured, but the second album was a disaster. It was not done at John's advantage because with Rod and I hurrying around the world it had to be done at our convenience.

PG: Of course the worst thing in the papers about you was the *Observer*'s comment about you and Liberace.

ELTON: I didn't see that.

PG: Do you want to hear it?

ELTON: Yes, Yes!

PG: It said that at the Royal Variety Performance Liberace made you look like the musical dwarf you were.

ELTON: Well, I think he did, I think he was the only decent thing on the Royal Variety Show. I don't mind, I don't find that offensive at all.

PG: You've also said Liberace was the only person who kept you sane at that.

55

ELTON: Oh, yes. We'd done that—oh, God, it was unbelievable. We were in the middle of a US tour and we flew from Los Angeles, just the band and my roadie and Larry Smith and my manager, and we flew into London Airport on a Sunday morning at the same time as the Osmonds and the Jackson Five. I was thinking "oh, let's get some nice English roast beef and a breakfast in a hotel." And we were besieged by people there. We rushed off from the hotel to the Palladium, we were there from about twelve o'clock to eight-thirty at night without any sleep and I was standing around feeling useless and the press was saying "why did you come to do the show?", "why did you break your American tour?" and I said "to plug my fucking record, that's why," because it was being seen on television, which wasn't the only reason, but it was true in a way because "Crocodile Rock" was just coming out. And also because I've never refused anything the Queen has asked me. The whole thing—I shared a dressing room with Jack Jones and Liberace. I had two numbers to do, which was really great, everybody was saying do "Your Song" and "Rocket Man", you better be nice, Elton John, and do "Your Song". Boring! So we brought "Legs" Larry to tap dance to "I Think I'm Gonna Kill Myself", and the whole effect was lost on television, but he released balloons that actually made farting noises. Of course the audience was full of the most dreadful people imaginable, and all these balloons were going "pffft, pfft, pfft", all over the

56

audience and they were all sitting there in their tiaras going "Ooooh! Oooooh!" (Bernie convulsed with laughter.)

Larry had all these flowers, because he came on dressed as a wedding man, and I thought it was great —it sounds abysmal—we thought we had problems, the poor Jackson Five singing, trying to sing without much amplification in the Palladium—and they were trying to get me to take Larry out of the show, and I was in a panic because I had to fly back to Tulsa to do another show. Liberace was great, he just kept wheeling trunks of clothes in. I just sat there watching him, he kept calm through the whole thing. All these people were badgering him all the time for autographs, and he does the most ornate autographs, he draws a grand piano, and he was great. He was really nice. He was the most professional person on that show. There were some really unprofessional people there, like Carol Channing. I mean, how dare she, how dare she walk on the same stage as me or anybody else? God, she was so pathetic! She really was, and everybody knew she was.

PG: How did you become involved with the National Youth Theatre?

ELTON: My solicitor said, would you like to go to the theatre, and I'm not a great theatre-goer. Whenever I go it usually turns out to be a bum play, something really awful. Just to be polite I said well, OK, I didn't really know where we were going, and he took me to a little theatre in London to see a play called *Good*

Lads at Heart, which is a story about a Borstal reform school. I was so knocked out, it had everything in it that everything else I'd ever seen lacked. I really became involved with it, I felt completely there. I said, this is great, what is the National Youth Theatre, and he told me he was the chairman of it. (Laughter.) He didn't hype me on it or anything, just came straight out with it. I said I've gotta do a concert for them, so we did three. One we did for the general public, which was a pound. One we charged five pounds for and Princess Margaret came and we deliberately sent around letters to all the people who should support things like that like EMI, and then we did one for kids around the country which was free, just for Youth Theatre members from everywhere. Then we did another one late in the year as well. They very generously made me Vice-President which I accepted, provided it wouldn't be just because I've raised an amount of money. I really try to be involved with it as I can, although I've missed three plays this year already because I'm not around, I don't have the chance. I sometimes go see them rehearse. It's just nice.

PG: About how many of Elton's shows do you go to now? I know you were at the birthday gig.

BERNIE: On the last tour I only saw three of them, the first one and the two at the Sundown [London]. It's very rare that I go to a British gig, unless it's in London and it's handy for me to get to. I tend to go to more of the American gigs, because if you're on the tour you go on all of it. On the last American tour I went to every place they played, which was fun. Tiring, but fun.

PG: You mention the London gigs. On this tour in London you had both the Imperial College and the Sundown Edmonton shows. Which audience do you prefer, the calmer college audience or the mass, sometimes younger audience?

ELTON: We try to play to a large cross-section of people, so we did a couple of university dates like Leeds and Imperial College, then we did ballrooms and theatres and then Edmonton, which is sort of like a big discotheque. I don't have any preferences. I get a little worried if you have screamers, if you have too many screamers it gets ridiculous. They usually keep quiet, if they scream they drive me around the bend. They generally listen, so I'm satisfied.

I find university audiences over here a bit tougher. People at Imperial College were nice, Leeds was *tough*. Perhaps they get a lot more entertainment, at prices they can afford. (Imitates an American commercial hypester.) "At prices *they* can afford."

Oh, well. I can play to anybody and I'm happy.

PG: The British pop press has made a big thing this tour of your having attracted a larger number of younger fans to the point where *Melody Maker* headlined that you've become a teen idol.

ELTON: Well, it's bound to happen to anyone who gets a hit single. Now the Strawbs get screamers. It would worry me if my whole audience was 13 year olds. I think the first five rows are the 13 year olds. I think we've always had people running down at the end, so I don't think it's anything new. At the moment everybody's gone mad on weenyboppers, and that's the word to freak out on. So it's the thing to call everybody a weenybop idol. It happens to anybody who has a hit, no matter if they're the ugliest people in the world. Look at me. If they scream at me, it's probably in horror.

BUSINESS TALK

PG: Why did you try to record in Jamaica?

ELTON: We went over there originally to record because although we usually record in France the Chateau had ground to a halt for a period of time because there was a dispute over who legally owned it. So we said, well, we'll go to Jamaica, the Stones have recorded there, the Staple Singers have. We booked the time, got equipment into the studio, it was all going very well, but there was never ever a sign of a good piano. They were always getting it the next day! There was only a five-foot Yamaha, which is fine banging away in the background of a Rolling Stones record, but for me a piano is very important. So it never appeared, and some other things never appeared, and we tried to get a sound together and couldn't. We weren't bitter about it, we knew there was going to be a risk when we went, and the band was going to fly home and I was going to go to New York, but they came in and said, what about our money, and the hotel people wouldn't let us go ... I've never been so pleased to leave anywhere as when we left Kingston.

PG: Do you think the stories of Jamaica being a

future focal point of recording have much validity?

ELTON: It could never be. Cat Stevens went over there—this was how disorganized it was, in a way—we had all the microphones and he was due to record in the small studio and we were due to record in the big studio. If he had come along as planned, he wouldn't have had anything at all. Luckily enough for him we split and he got along OK. There's no reason why it shouldn't be a good place, but just for us it was a disaster.

PG: How did the Chateau start?

ELTON: My solicitor said "you've got to start recording outside the country" and I said "why?" and he said it would be much better financially if we recorded outside the country. I said "you must be joking." He wasn't. So I said I'd go only if we could find some place peaceful without any interruptions. We started getting a dossier on all European studios and this Chateau leaflet came through. It looked ideal, forty kilometers north of Paris in the middle of nowhere, swimming pool, food, lodging, tennis court—and it is, we went over and it has an atmosphere all its own. I love it. You can record in a room with a thirteenth century chandelier overlooking nothing but fields. You've got a room to rehearse in, you just take the band upstairs and you're in the studio.

BERNIE: It's the ideal concept for recording. You're totally cut off, so there's no way people can ring you, there's nobody pestering you. You can just eat, sleep

62

and record, at your own leisure.

ELTON: It can become a bit of a routine, getting up the same time every day. After awhile it drives you mad.

BERNIE: I've been able to sort that out by not going until the last few days, because it can get on top of you unless you're actually in the studio. If I had something constructive to do it wouldn't be so bad, but it doesn't knock me out to just sit around watching people work in the studio. I come at the last possible week.

ELTON: When we made *Don't Shoot Me* he hadn't heard any of the songs, he had given me the lyrics and was in America. Usually I play them to him but this time he just came over and heard the album more or less as it stood.

BERNIE: It was really strange. Usually I give him the lyrics and he plays me them, but this time I flew in on a big silver bird and just heard the tracks, which had never happened before. I wouldn't want to do that again because it was weird.

PG: Bernie just mentioned how at the Chateau it's nice not to be pestered. Have you reached the stage where that's becoming a real problem in your life?

ELTON: Currently it is. You can't go anywhere without people gawking at you. I didn't mind people who come up to you, but people who just stand there and go "Ooooohlooooo", I mean, what can you do? You just stand there and go red, at least I do. I just think it's a passing phase. I don't mind people—autographs are a stupid habit, whoever invented that with scrawny paper, I mean, it's alright if you're Rembrandt or Picasso, but I think it's stupid. I do it, signing this one to Shirley and this one to Colin, but it gets you down sometime. Sometimes people don't realize you need a bit of privacy.

PG: That night in the Royal Festival Hall, the Bee Gees concert.

ELTON: I just felt so embarrassed that night, it's very strange, but you can *feel* everybody's eyes on you. I suppose I've put myself into a position where I have to live with it. It's like when you go see the Queen— well, of course, she's used to it, she handles it very well.

PG: With these circumstances, do you go to many shows or not?

ELTON: I'm not going to let myself become a hermit because of it. I'm not going to stay in. I'm going to see Roxy Music on Sunday at the Rainbow. It's such a terrible building, I prefer the Edmondton Sundown any time, it's got atmosphere. You walk in the place and you feel the atmosphere. You walk into the Rainbow and you say, fuck, what a dump.

PG: At the Sundown did you mind the kids being lifted up on stage? [With no seats on the ground floor, girls were constantly being passed over people's heads onto the stage to be carried off.]

ELTON: It is sort of disconcerting when you're in the middle of "Mona Lisas and Mad Hatters" and your eyes are closed and you can sense eighteen ton ladies being lifted past you.

PG: Everyone in the press seemed to get a kick out of keeping count.

ELTON: Well, the second night was the worst. Most of them are real fainters. One girl, though, was being lifted backstage and out of the corner of her eye she saw Rod Stewart and went "AAAAAAH! ROD STEWART!" Obviously some are let's-get-back-stagers. They're so strong, those women, you see one of them coming towards you, you think, that's it, you're in for a wrestle, because they're determined not to let you go, whether it's hair or fingernails they've got a hold of.

PG: You were quoted recently as saying you'd one day like to do an album of your own stuff but inevitably it would turn out gloomy.

ELTON: I think it would. I like writing songs like "First Episode at Heinton", which really doesn't have any shape or form, it just meandered with a general feel of wistfulness. I'd love to eventually, I feel I could write lyrics someday, I might want to, but I just can't see it happening imminently.

PG: "Talking Old Soldiers" was rather unusual in being almost a narrative.

ELTON: That was a very David Ackles influenced song. If you notice *Tumbleweed Connection* is dedicated "with love to David". That's David Ackles. It is sort of a narrative.

PG: You don't do the transcriptions for sheet music of your songs.

ELTON: Oh, no. I can't, I'm not capable of doing that. I just make the record and leave that up to the people who are paid to do it, forty pounds a week or whatever.

PG: There has been critical controversy concerning Paul Buckmaster's correct role in your recordings. In there being a little instrumental overkill on *Madman*, for example.

ELTON: That was an album of frustrations for everybody, we were all going through heavy stages. Paul was getting . . . well, he's very strange, Paul, he can't work under pressure. We were *all* under pressure, because we had to get that fucking album going. I don't know how that album ever got out. When we were doing the actual track "Madman Across the Water", for example, Paul arrived with no score! There were sixty string musicians sitting there and we had to scrap it. There were all those sort of disasters.

But overall I don't think Paul has gotten the credit he deserves. He's influenced so many string writers, especially the *Elton John* album, everybody pinches off Paul Buckmaster. Like Lennon on *Imagine*, I'm not saying he pinched it, but he used a lot of strings on "How Do You Sleep?" I think nobody really used strings until Buckmaster came along and showed them you can use strings without having them being sugary and awful. I think Jack Nitzche's arrangement on the Neil Young is very Buckmasterish.

BERNIE: What, on *Harvest*? I thought they were disgusting, those arrangements, they just crucified those songs. They were like, yeccch.

ELTON: We searched. I'd never heard of Paul before. There wasn't one arranger in the world I liked except for Jimmy Webb, and you can't get a word out of him, he's so introspective. I think if [John] McLaughlin arranged something it would be great. But then I think he could do anything.

Buckmaster, if he got himself together, and he's not together at all, if he got himself together he could eat them *all* for breakfast, because he's got so many ideas. He's just done that Ringo film, but you can't pressurize him, he's so slow. I think most arrangers are fucking awful, dreadful, dreary.

PG: You obviously admire McLaughlin. Who else currently do you like?

BERNIE: I can never answer that, my mind always goes blank. I think it boils down to what you're playing at the moment.

ELTON: I like Stealers Wheel.

BERNIE: I was just going to say that, I like that a lot. And Joni Mitchell, the longer she's been around the more she's grown on me. I was playing that album today again in the car, *For the Roses*, I just find myself playing that all the time. Fucking incredible album. She sees so brilliantly. She's a genius. There are a lot of different standards as far as lyricists are concerned, I wouldn't say I'm the same kind as Joni Mitchell is, but on her level there is nobody who can touch her. The more I listen to her the more phenomenal she gets. Some of the lines she writes. I could go on for hours just thinking of lines of hers.

ELTON: I like Stevie Wonder. I usually wind up playing the same old tapes in the car.

BERNIE: There are four things I can think of offhand that I play all the time. Joni Mitchell, Stealers Wheel, the Johnny Nash, which is my favorite album, and the Beach Boys album I play at lot.

ELTON: I can't stand that! Dreadful . . . and I love the Beach Boys. I play the Joan Armatrading a lot. I like the Stylistics and people like that.

BERNIE: I still like Jesse Winchester. I wish somebody would do something for him, he's got a great voice.

ELTON: Trouble is he has to record in Canada.

BERNIE: I've bought so many albums in the last few weeks and the majority of it's crap.

PG: As we mentioned in the car the American and British charts have rarely been so different. Do you as a rule prefer the songs that become popular in Britain or in America?

ELTON: The American chart. In England it's boring. If you're Marc Bolan or Slade or even Tyrannasaurus Rex or Donny Osmond or any of the Osmonds you come leaping into the chart at number three. I used to like some of Slade's things, but I think they've really gone down the path.

BERNIE: I like putting out singles now. I think we're really putting out good singles.

ELTON: I prefer the American chart this week. I mean, let's compare. (Gets copy of charts.) I get *Billboard*, *Record World*, and *Cashbox*. OK, British chart.

Gilbert O'Sullivan's record ["Get Down"] is great, right? The Timmy Thomas is a great record. "Feel the Need in Me" by the Detroit Emeralds wasn't a hit in the States, that's a good record. "Pyjamarama" is a good record that won't make it in the States, "Cindy Incidentally" is a good record . . .

BERNIE: You told me "Cindy Incidentally" was dreadful.

ELTON: That grew on me. Their records always do. Those are the best kind, really.

BERNIE: I never get tired of Rod's records. Whenever I'm driving and I need to hear a good record I pop in one of Rod's albums. And he's another great writer, he comes up with so many great lines.

ELTON: You get so much dreck in the English charts. How many records are dreck? Let's see. [Going from the top down.] Donny Osmond is dreck, Slade I don't like, Dawn, Shirley Bassey, Kenny, Alice Cooper, "Nice One, Cyril" is double dreck, New Seekers is dreck, Dave Edmunds is dreck compared to the Ronnettes, Gladys Knight and the Pips, why they ever released "The Look of Love" I'll never know, there's just *so much dreck*. Then you come to the American charts, the new Gladys Knight, which is superb, Edward Bear, oh, that's dreck, the Carpenters double, double dreck, Vickie Lawrence *treble* dreck, that's even worse, Dawn's there, Dr. Hook Bernie likes, "Dead Skunk"—well, now, if Loudon Wainwright III can have a hit in America, there's hope! "Space Oddity", five years too late . . . on the radio in America he was interviewed and said "everyone is saying Elton had a hit with 'Rocket Man' because you did 'Space Oddity'," and he said, "well, you said it." Now I say that David Bowie's having a hit with "Space Oddity" because I had "Rocket Man" and paved the way for him. "Cisco Kid", I mean, just so many better records on the American chart, of course I'm a soul freak ... there's Stealers Wheel ... "Walk on the Wild Side"! Now if *that* can be a hit in America! Jud Strunk, Donna Fargo, some good records there ... "Crocodile Rock" steaming down the chart at the rate of twenty-two places a week ... [Elton and Bernie debate who is worse, David Cassidy or Donny Osmond, for three minutes. Elton defends Cassidy.]

BERNIE: What was that letter you got?

ELTON: Oh, I got a letter saying that compared to David Cassidy I looked like a hedgehog.

PG: What about one person I know you like, Dusty Springfield?

ELTON: She's another person who needs desperately to have someone get a hold of her and say "don't record that". She's made three albums in a row now which have been terrible, not musically, just that they're musak. She's so capable. *Dusty in Memphis* was one of the all-time good albums. She should be recording Stylistics type material.

BERNIE: Slagging time, folks!

ELTON: No, it's true, it's very sad when someone who is that good, a very good singer of songs, dynamite on stage . . . She's capable of much better, and it really frustrates me, and it must frustrate her more. Her new album is disgusting, it has no balls to it, Dusty needs something with balls.

BERNIE: [Bizarre animal noises.]

ELTON: No, it's true for a lot of people. Ray Charles hasn't made a decent record for about five years. Those album covers, I mean, because the poor guy's blind they give him the worst album covers. Have you seen that new one, the mauve thing with the black glasses? Horrible!

BERNIE: I'd like to make a record with Gene Pitney. I think Gene Pitney has a great voice.

PG: Do you think you, Elton, could ever work with Dusty?

ELTON: I've certainly made enough hints. But she went and signed with ABC-Dunhill. I would produce her, but I don't want to produce for bloody ABC-Dunhill, I don't like them.

PG: You've taken great care to give credit to the members of the band both on stage and on albums. Some people don't do that.

ELTON: That's because I think they're great and I want them to be able to continue after we've stopped playing together. You can be a fantastic bass player for Free and then Free breaks up and you have to start off all over again fairly anonymously with a new group in some obscure places. I don't want that to happen to Davey, Dee and Nigel. They're too good. When we stop, I hope wherever they go they will be known for their own work straight away.

PG: Speaking of break-ups, in January you were bemoaning how business interferes with music and pointed to *Apple to the Core*, the story of the Beatles' break-up, as evidence. Of course Dick James was involved in that book. How has he fared? With you?

ELTON: I think he's made his fair share out of me. I know he invested a lot of money in the beginning. I will say one thing for him, you do get royalty statements from him. I can always go down and audit his books and things like that. I think he's been a little unfair on the publishing side of things. I don't think we've gotten screwed as a lot of other people have. He's made a lot of money out of me, but he's got a gift for making money, so that's fair enough.

PG: Bernie, do you take much interest in the financial end?

BERNIE: Uhh ... yeah, if my money doesn't come through! (Laughter.) No, not particularly, I don't understand business. People are in business for business, that's all you can say, really.

ELTON: DJM Records have been a bloody good little record company. They've done me proud. We were one of the first pop acts to be advertised on television, with *Tumbleweed Connection*, and they've televised ads for *Don't Shoot Me*. Now everybody's advertising on television.

They've always given me the covers I want, they've always been—well, even though we had a hassle with them over "Daniel", they put it out, where they could have just said "forget it". They were in their legal rights to stop it. So I think we've done better with DJM than anybody else. I have no grouses against them. They've been far better for me, in terms of creative work, than MCA. MCA in the States put my albums out in shoddy covers, which I don't like very much. In their advertising, they don't take any thought into it. They put me out like a kind of soap, they don't really care about the creative side of things. I mean, the *Don't Shoot Me* album cover in America is disgusting, really bad.

PG: One of the adverts in the American trades MCA put in they called the album "the latest adventures of Reg and Bernie in France."

ELTON: I was so furious, so furious. And that was stuck in a row of cabbages. (Bernie laughs.) It was at the top of the album output. It was the week the album went to number one as well, which really infuriated me. It was stuck on the top of a page of albums which to say the least weren't that distinctive. We were stuck in with Loretta Lynn and . . .

BERNIE: Dobie Gray. (Laughter.)

ELTON: Dobie Gray and all that lot. I mean I don't mind, but I always thought the company was very Neil Diamond-orientated. He probably thinks the company's been very Elton John-orientated. He gets good ads, he gets color ads, because he's over there and he gets to pressure them more. I just think they're very lacksadaisical. They probably think "he really won't mind" but I resent it, I think I must be the only person in the world who delivers their album on time. When *Honky Chateau* was the number one album they knew the next one was in the can, and they'd heard it. I really don't see they've got much to complain about me. It sounds like I'm having a go at them, but it really hurts me when we take that much trouble, I think our album sleeves and everything are just so important, and they bung them out and they're shitty and they really don't mind. They don't seem to think I'll care. "Well, after we've done it, he can't really complain."

But basically we've had a good understanding with MCA. Let's face it, we're one of the few things they've got. They've got Sonny and Cher and Neil Diamond catalog and fuck-all else. The Who, sorry, and a very good country catalog, and nothing else. Of course there's a good relationship, who wouldn't in their position? We put Rocket, our own label, with them because we've had a good relationship with MCA, I'm not putting them down, but they just need booting up the ass every now and then.

PG: Which leads us to Rocket. What exactly is your plan with it? When did you first think about it and whose idea was it?

ELTON: It was conceived when we were doing *Don't Shoot Me*, right?

BERNIE: In France, the idea came about, because Davey was going to make an album and he hadn't got a label to go out on.

74

ELTON: We went to a lot of companies—I didn't, John Reid and Steve Brown did—where the artist would get a decent deal if the album were to become successful. We didn't ask for the world, but nobody would give us a reasonable deal. We went to EMI, everybody. So we were sitting around the table saying, what are we going to do, and I think it was me, actually, who said "start our own fucking label!" because we'd all been drinking wine, the Chateau produces its own wine. We all said "Yeah!" and then went to bed and we all got up the next morning and said "was everybody serious?" We all decided we were, so it all started as a result of Davey Johnstone, and nothing else. After hearing Davey's album, which has taken a year to get together, not for lack of work but because he hasn't had much studio time, those people are really going to kick themselves, because it's a fucking masterful album. That's how it started.

I mean, I've always dreamed of having my own record company. As a kid I used to watch the 78s when the labels were beautiful to look at, I'd watch them go round. I'm fascinated by records. Anything on London was boring, or EMI, because of those plain labels. Now what used to have good labels? (Thinks for a few seconds.) Polydor was quite interesting . . .

BERNIE: There's a picture of James Brown now on his records.

ELTON: The five of us involved sat down—Bernie and I, Steve Brown, who handles the A&R side, John

Reid and Gus Dudgeon, who does production, although Bernie and I will be doing production as well, Steve and John will basically handle the business side, and we just set out to cultivate new talent. MCA gave us a good advance, but that's more or less gone in finding offices, staff, and decorating the offices. We can't go out and pay $50,000 in advance and therefore we can't sign any name acts. We didn't particularly want to, anyway. It's very odd, we're just trying to find people from scratch. We're going to give a fair deal and a better royalty rate than they could get from WEA. Plus the fact that Steve Brown is the most amazing person, you should do an interview with him. It's like a family, you know. I know it's very idyllic and the Moody Blues have done it and the Beatles did it, but I really think Rocket will be something different. The good thing about it is I'm not on it. It would be hopeless from the start. It would dampen everybody else. It's like the Moody Blues are on Threshold, and so are Trapeze. It would be Elton John is on Rocket, and so are Longdancer and Davey Johnstone. Longdancer are not mindshattering yet, but most of them are only eighteen. They've got a long way to go. It's hard to find mindshattering talent just like that. If you've got mindshattering talent, you want a million dollars for it.

It's just a thing we've started quietly, I don't think there's been too much hype about it. I think Davey's album will be successful, at least from a critical standpoint, a la Joan Armatrading's album. It's fucking brilliant. Longdancer's album is very good for a first album, sort of an *Empty Sky* album, very raw and basic. And Bernie and I are producing Kiki Dee, who's been around for a long time, living in the wake of Dusty Springfield, really, gradually fading into the background, and she could sing the balls off Rita Coolidge any day. We're trying to write a special song for her, we've never ever done that for anybody else, to try to get her off the ground, to try to get her publicity and everything. Bernie's task is really hard because he's got to write one as a girl. So he slips into Maxine's dresses every morning . . . (both laugh).

REFLECTIONS ON THEIR LIFE

PG: The general critical response to *Don't Shoot Me* was that it represented the end of the three-year critical rise and fall and rise of Elton John. Do you think that's fair?

ELTON: I don't know about *Don't Shoot Me*. I think it's a weird sort of album. I suppose it's fair to say the rise and the fall and the rise again——

BERNIE: Where was the fall?

ELTON: Everyone's got this myth about the fall. The fall is probably because of *Madman Across the Water*. It didn't get into the top ten or top twenty, but it still sold 65,000 albums in England, which isn't bad. I think because we didn't have a single out for a year and a half people thought we were dead, but the album still did very well everywhere else in the world. So that was the "fall", as it were.

BERNIE: I think there's a lull in everybody's career. You can rise with tremendous popularity and then everybody sort of jumps on your back. They're writing everything about you and you get to a stage where people want to see if you can maintain that popularity and the press coverage goes down slightly during a phase when you're trying to change your

78

. . .and for 'Goodbye Yellow Brick Road'

At home...

PHOTOGRAPH: BARRIE WENTZELL

...and in concert at Edmunton.

Elton and Bernie, then.

Bernie and Elton, now.

*Elton John in concert at the
Edmunton Sundown theatre, 1974.*

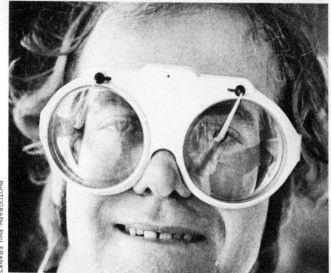

*At home with part of his collection
of gold discs, gifts and awards...
and a pair of glasses with wipers.*

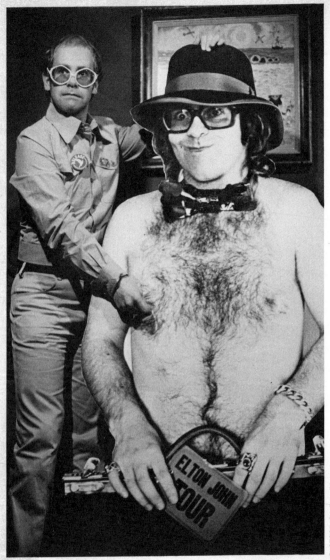

Elton and friend.

system of doing things and you have to come back. That's like crossing the bridge. You either cross it or you fall off it.

ELTON: We go through spates where for six months you're acclaimed and then for six months you're not and we've learned to ride with it now. We're very very popular at the moment, we've got the press on our side with *Don't Shoot Me*. I'm surprised, I thought *Don't Shoot Me* would get ripped apart——

PG: Why?

ELTON: Because I think it's a very happy album, very ultra-pop, if you look at any of our other albums it's very poppy, just very straight pop. I don't think there'll be another *Don't Shoot Me* album from me. The reason it came out like this was we'd done *Honky Chateau* and were really knocked out with it and everyone was so happy that the songs came out that way. It was just done with a tremendous amount of energy. Don't you agree it's a very sort of poppy album?

BERNIE: I was thinking ...

ELTON: I always think of it as Elton John's disposable album.

BERNIE: Well, as you said before, a lot of times it's good to write disposable songs. You can write one or two "classics", that will last and be covered again in a few years time, but I think a majority of good pop songs nowadays are disposable. They're songs for the time they're in the charts and three months later they're just completely forgotten and nobody bothers with them again. I think that's healthy in a way. You should always have fresh material coming along.

ELTON: Like the time *Elton John* was recorded we had all the stuff ready for *Tumbleweed* so those albums were really easy to make because we had a stockpile and *Don't Shoot Me* and *Honky* followed in the same sort of way. We had all the stuff, sort of a stockpile after not having had one for *Madman*, which was really an effort to get out, when it was really a pain to try to get nine or ten numbers together. This situation has been sorted out now because we've always been prolific, except for the time when I was nearly worked to death.

BERNIE: Exactly. The reason we've survived and will continue to survive for a good long time is because we've got the upper hand on everybody else and can turn our ideas into anything, any sort of music. We can do things like just playing rock and roll, twelve bars, to country material, blues ... I mean, we've done every type of music. You could compile an album taking tracks from all the things we've done and come across with the most amazing cross-section of material.

ELTON: We're influenced by so many things. You could say I'm the Ray Coniff of the pop world. You know what I mean?

BERNIE: But other people who are sort of on the same level of popularity tend to have the same feel on all their albums.

80

ELTON: A Neil Young or a Carole King or a James Taylor album all have the same sort of thing. They do it for three or four albums getting away with having the same sound. We've never had an album that had the same sound.

BERNIE: It's amazing that the Moody Blues can release an album every six months and bang, straight to number one, it's like listening to the same album again. It amazed me a while ago when people said our things sounded the same and that we should get out of a rut. That's really strange. Why pick on us? Why not pick on somebody like Jethro Tull where it's always the same sort of line-up, the same sort of construction of the song, the same feel. Not that that's bad, I like Jethro Tull.

ELTON: With all due respect to Carole King, *Tapestry* was a great album, but the other two albums after that sounded like they were recorded at the same sessions but that *Tapestry* was the first ten tracks done and the next twenty were done when everyone was getting increasingly more tired. She should worry, though, having written some of the world's great songs, but I couldn't work with that same line-up on every album.

BERNIE: I think that's important to get across, because some people——

ELTON: I get fucking pissed off at people saying "their songs always sound the same". How can you say "Have Mercy on the Criminal" sounds like "Daniel" or "Daniel" sounds like "High Flying Bird".

BERNIE: Somebody once said that "Burn Down the Mission" sounded like "Friends". (Laughter.) That's true, that's an actual quote from a paper.

ELTON: Someone said I sounded like Joe Cocker, which I thought was rather amusing. I can see Jose Feliciano, but not Joe Cocker.

BERNIE: That Jose Feliciano thing has sort of levelled out now, it was just around . . .

ELTON: Well, they were saying Elton John sounds like Jose Feliciano, now Jose Feliciano sounds like Elton John. I mean, isn't that stupid? Actually, I sound like the Mills Brothers. No, Doris Day.

PG: Doris Day's "Que Sera, Sera" was number one on the BBC's all-time most requested list.

ELTON: Along with "How Much is That Doggie in the Window . . . "

BERNIE: And "Laughing Policeman . . . "

PG: And "My Way."

BERNIE: Well, that's a newie, that.

PG: On the way over we were talking about how some performers need only a couple of hits and they are sustained as far as live appearances and attendances go, whereas other people live or die on the basis of their current release. Do you think that together you'll be in a position where you're judged just on the success of your latest record?

ELTON: I think you always are. I think if you release a stiff record you're gonna get . . . I mean, anyone can release a flop. We've done it.

PG: What was your flop?

ELTON: Well, I think the live album was a flop, compared to anything else we've ever done. It got up to I think about nine on the *Billboard* chart, but it only sold about 220,000 which isn't much compared to what we have sold. So that was a flop at the time when it should have been a monstrous seller. And also we've had singles, I mean "Friends" wasn't exactly a big hit. "Honky Cat" was a flop over here, that was my fault.

PG: Why was it your fault?

ELTON: I saw it steaming up the American charts, it sold more than "Rocket Man" in America I think, so I said "we're mad, we're mad, we're sitting on a hit", so I said "it must come out, it must come out" and we released it with "Lady Samantha" and "It's Me That You Need", two deleted tracks, made it a maxi-single, and it got to 31 in England. It was very embarrassing.

BERNIE: It was a while after *Honky Chateau* had been released over here and everybody already had the album. In America it's different, you can take tracks off an album and they'll be hits, but you can't do that here.

ELTON: The Stylistics had five hits off that bloody album . . . Johnny Nash has had two——

BERNIE: No, three. (Elton's mother brings in tea and biscuits.)

ELTON: Well done, Mom . . . I think there's always somebody ready to step in who's in your corner of the market. I think people who buy our records buy Cat Stevens and Paul Simon. I don't think we're in the same category as the Blue Oyster Cult or Black Oak Arkansas. If there is a hot singer-songwriter, like Don McLean was very hot for awhile, kids who can't afford to buy two records might buy Don McLean's record instead of mine. It was the time of *Madman* that people were buying Carole King and Cat Stevens. I don't think you can say that anybody is safe these days with a record. One of the Beatles, maybe, not even the Stones are safe, I think only the Beatles can release something and it will automatically be a monster.

PG: Well, that's not true, really, because Lennon has bombed.

ELTON: I meant the Beatles as the Beatles...I suppose you're right. I don't really count *New York City*, I just act as if it never existed. I look at my albums and I really want them to sell because we put so much effort into our stuff, we really do. I don't think we can say "well, we'll just bang an album out and it'll sell because we always sell a lot of albums." If we really did that, if we sat down and said our contract demands an album by such-and-such, and we put out an album of shitty stuff, sub-standard stuff, I don't think it would sell that well. I think the proof of the pudding is the Lennon album. There you go.

PG: Bernie said he felt he became truly confident he could trust you with a song during *Tumbleweed*. When did you get that feeling?

ELTON: I've always had it. I've never worried about it. From *Honky* onwards he's been saying things so much simpler. Especially the new one he's gotten into his stride. It's as if *Madman* was the last of that sort of song, and now the *Honky* era is finished and we're starting on a new thing. That's the way I see it. There's a song called "Sweet Painted Ladies", which is a song about ladies who satisfy seamen who come to port. "Forget us, we'll be gone very soon / Forget we ever slept in your room / And we'll leave the smell of the sea in your bed / Where love's just a job and nothing is said." That's great.

BERNIE: It really has a Noel Coward type of treatment, which is a strange combination, a song about whores and a Noel Coward sound. [Sir Noel had died five days previous.]

PG: Are you as fond of "Candle in the Wind" as Bernie is?

ELTON: Yes. There's a whole set of songs we've already written. "Candle in the Wind" is one, then "Goodbye Yellow Brick Road" and one called "I've Seen That Movie, Too". With "Sweet Painted Ladies", we have four really classy songs. If we could ever record an album as good as *Abbey Road*, I'd want to retire. Even though it's not my favorite Beatles album, you hear "Something" and "Here Comes the Sun" and you want to fall down. Usually somebody has one good song on an album, but the Beatles had five or six mind-blowers. So this is the way I feel about our next one. It's strange, you can compare against the Beatles, *Revolver* lifted them onto a higher plane, and I think *Honky* did that for us, and then *Sgt. Pepper* was their most popular and *Don't Shoot Me* was ours, and then they had the white album, and now we'll have a double, too.

PG: Do you look at it the same way or do you get that analytical about the albums?

BERNIE: After *Don't Shoot Me* I really wanted the next album to be not leaning so much on the production side, with a looser, more spontaneous feel to it . . . an album where if there's a false ending, or someone shouts something, you can keep it in. I love *Let It Be* because it's got that. The production and sound are there, but you're not aware of it. Those things Leon Russell had on the first album, those sort of fake beginnings where things went wrong, they were really effective, I like things like that.

ELTON: We're going to take more time on this album than on any previous one. Usually it takes about eight days with two more days for overdubs.

BERNIE: I'm not very high on strings right now——

ELTON: I like strings as floaters now, not as lead instruments. Like when the strings come in on the Joan Armatrading album, it just send shivers up my spine. They're just there, you don't notice them, they're just going "rrrrrrrrrrrrrr", it's just an amazing sound.

BERNIE: What do you foresee strings on on the new album?

ELTON: Maybe "Goodbye Yellow Brick Road". You can't really tell until you've laid the tracks down. We can say "Candle in the Wind" will be a single and then in the studio something else might turn out to be much stronger. When we went to record *Honky Chateau* we thought "Salvation" would be the single.

RAMBLING MEN

ELTON: Davey and I were driving after one of the gigs on the tour and we had had a couple of drinks in the car [which is chauffeured] and we put this new Dory Previn album on. Have you listened to that? Davey and I were in hysterics, we were laughing so hard. Not *at* it ... I don't know what it was ... it was like the first time I ever heard Leonard Cohen, I couldn't stop listening.

BERNIE: But you were laughing. Why?

ELTON: Well, these songs, nobody's ever written any songs like them. There's this song about her being left-handed and going to a nun's school where they said you can't be left-handed, so she wrote this song about being changed from left-handed to right-handed because it wasn't natural. We were sitting there listening to it and it drove us around the bend, nearly. I really love it. I mean, she can't sing, forget it, but this is really something.

BERNIE: How about the song on *Mythical Kings and Iguanas* with the zeppelin blowing up with her father in it——

PG: Remember, she's had some hard times.

ELTON: I've never heard anybody so original in years.

There's something about her, not her voice and not her lyrics, which are very basic, which makes you unable to stop listening to her. I've got to take that album to Italy, because I think I'm going to fall in love with that.

BERNIE: I can't play her at home because she drives Maxine mad.

ELTON: You've got to listen to this one. Are you coming to Italy at all?

BERNIE: No.

ELTON: Bastard.

BERNIE: See you in France!

ELTON: I've become a legend in Italy because I never turn up.

PG: You've had two tours cancelled there.

ELTON: Right on the day before. There's a competition in Italy, is he going to turn up or isn't he? And more people are voting for he isn't than he is. The promoter's lost all credibility. Both times it's been genuine. First Nigel put his back out and then I was on the verge of a nervous breakdown the second time. I made *Don't Shoot Me* really on the verge of a nervous breakdown. I was so ill. I didn't know it, but I had glandular fever and was very slow. I was in a very peculiar mood when I made that album. When we first went over to make it *Honky Chateau* had just gone to number one in the States and I said to Gus, "I can't make this album," so he said, "alright, we'll do it in September." Then I said to myself, wait, I'm going on holiday in July, it would be nice to have it over with by then. It's a terrible way to look at it, but I thought it would be terrible to have come all the way over and not do it and have it out of the way. So we did it although I was very ill and had some terrible rows. I don't think Dick James and I spoke to each other for four months after that.

BERNIE: I came over to France and you didn't know I was coming, did you?

ELTON: No.

BERNIE: He found me under a bush!

ELTON: He'd flown in from Los Angeles and hid behind a bush! I walked out on the lawn in the morning——

BERNIE: I wasn't hiding, I was just sitting there——

ELTON: He'd been phoning up every night from Los Angeles and the next morning I come out and there he is behind a bloody bush. In France! Nearly sent me around the bend.

BERNIE: Didn't mean to.

ELTON: Now you know what it was like flying in for that Royal Variety Show and then flying out again like nothing was happening.

PG: Do you plan on touring any place other than Italy? And, eventually, America?

ELTON: I plan on taking a department-by-department tour of Harrod's.

BERNIE: A tour of Brixton?

ELTON: No, the only thing planned is the recording and a holiday for me in July. Then we'll probably do a tour of the States late in the year, go to Japan and

90

Australia beginning of next year——

BERNIE: I dread spending a month in LA. I have visions of all those trunks and everything——

ELTON: I always have a sojourn to Los Angeles every year and last year we had a house in Malibu, and we took Bryan Forbes and his kids. We're such great looters, Bernie and Maxine and I, that they needed a Greyhound bus to take us to the airport. There were sixty-seven cases and there must have been thirty-two of those trunks, you know those Newberry's trunks with the American flag on them?

BERNIE: The most amazing thing about that was it cost us a hundred quid to get them out of customs. Thousands and thousands of dollars worth of records and books, and it cost us a hundred quid to get them through.

ELTON: We used to get up in the morning and go, "right, here we go, looting." Bryan would go with Bernie to a bookshop and I'd go to a tablecloth shop and we all had such a laugh. But sixty-seven suitcases. The guy who owned the house freaked out. Sixty-seven suitcases, it sounds like Liberace. I never do a tour of America without coming back with about eight more suitcases. I have in that loft up there about forty suitcases. I don't know what to do with them.

PG: Of course you don't have the room for them.

BERNIE: That's why I've got to get a new house——

ELTON: *I* haven't got the room! So God knows what Bernie is doing.

BERNIE: It's just murder, there's an overflow.

ELTON: I've got to build. The dining room has a flat roof so I can build out above it, which is quite nice.

PG: Does Maxine suggest you go to the States often?

BERNIE: She doesn't have to, really, we go over so often, and I love LA. I've really thought seriously of living there. For the amount of money it would take to buy a house here, I could buy a fucking great mansion in Bel Air. It's quite tempting, but LA works on you in strange ways. It can very easily turn you crazy. You've seen it destroy people. But if you don't live there, if you regulate the amount of time you spend there, it's great.

ELTON: It's a great place to arrive in and it's a great place to leave. I always feel good when I'm leaving it.

BERNIE: I lived there for three months once and I found it really begins to get into your blood——

ELTON: To slow you down——

BERNIE: It was frightening to feel "I've *got* to get out of here".

ELTON: It slowed me down. No wonder there aren't many prolific song-writers there.

BERNIE: I couldn't work there.

ELTON: All you do is get up at twelve o'clock, go sit by the pool, have a few drinks—I couldn't stand that.

BERNIE: If you're in the right frame of mind, it's fun, there are so many good shops. So Maxine gets over there often enough.

ELTON: New York's a great looter's paradise, too, all those shops. Bernie goes looking for posters.

PG: You do have a lot of Marilyn Monroe artifacts, don't you?

BERNIE: Yes, I've just had a load of stuff framed. I don't know where I'm going to put them, though. I think Marilyn was so misunderstood, people kept trying to make her what she wasn't. ["Candle in the Wind" is about Marilyn.]

PG: And Elton, you were talking in the car about the two Rembrandts and the Durer.

ELTON: Oh, Bernie, that's right. Two Rembrandt etchings, from Harrod's. And John [Reid] bought a Rembrandt etching two inches by one inch on H.P.!

BERNIE: (Laughter.) On H.P.!

ELTON: You can buy them on H.P. You should go in there and invest in them.

BERNIE: How much do they cost?

ELTON: The cheapest you can get is about two thousand. But they go up in price so much. I bought mine for a start, one was £7,000, one was £5,000. They're just amazing to look at, you don't know which one to have.

BERNIE: How come all these are for sale?

ELTON: Harrod's got a large quantity in. About twenty. The Japanese are getting all the rest. Harrod's went to an auction and the bloody Japanese were buying them. I didn't know there were any Rembrandts left. Then there's a Renoir on wrapping paper that's soul-destroying, that was £12,500. There's another Rembrandt, a landscape of three trees and a landscape, which is no bigger than that [makes tiny shape with fingers], but you need a magnifying glass. A fucking big magnifying glass! I never dreamed there were Rembrandts still to buy, I thought they were all in museums. You should invest, really, they're such a great investment. Well, I have no Picassos because I don't particularly like Picasso. I do like his pottery, though. I love art nouveau posters, and I like posters in general. I just buy out of pleasure. I'd rather have a picture or a painting than anything else. I have a lot of expensive posters, but I have a cheap old Bette Midler poster down there that wasn't even for sale but I liked it.

PG: How does your mom feel about all this stuff?

ELTON: My dad hates it, he has to hang them all. My mom likes them, she says the place looks like a museum. I mean, I don't think she likes half the stuff, she's a bit cheap there (Bernie laughs), she's got her own tastes——

BERNIE: I buy books on the American West. There's this bookshop in New York who has these great first editions about people like Wyatt Earp and Billy the Kid. I've got a book written by Emmett Dalton, signed by Emmett Dalton, and it's my prized possession.

ELTON: In the bathroom I've got this drawing of me and Groucho Marx and he's signed it "Marx Groucho" because he says my name is backwards. That's one of *my* prized possessions. The people I admire most are legends like him and Mae West. In America, when she walked in, I couldn't say anything. I was completely in awe. I still don't really believe I met her, she's a figment of the imagination, that woman.

PG: Did you see where Alice Cooper gave a "Living Legend" plaque to George Burns?

ELTON: George Burns made a great quote in that article. "I was four years ahead of my time and one thing you don't need to be at my age is four years ahead of my time." There were a couple of great quotes. Alice Cooper himself, he must get so tired, he never stops.

BERNIE: That tour must kill him, I'm sure.

ELTON: Well, I've done fifty-five cities, but——

BERNIE: The theatrics and the setting-up——

ELTON: He really does get bruised. I saw him at the Hollywood Bowl and he came down to the beach house the next day and his leg was cut up all where he had that fight. They really go into him. He must be a wreck.

BERNIE: Oh, but I like him, though.

ELTON: He really had it down well.

BERNIE: Good lad. He can really sink a few frosties.

ELTON: I was in awe there, I was a fan, and when the helicopter came over and dropped the paper panties there I was, scrambling for them. And the posters they were throwing about, too. It was great to be a fan and be normal again.

BERNIE: I remember you going "Oooooooooh!"

ELTON: I *did* get a pair of panties. *And* a poster, which I gave to my cousin. I like him, he's really down-to-earth.

BERNIE: I never see a picture of him where he doesn't have a can of beer in his hand.

ELTON: I smashed him in table tennis and there was this thing in *Rolling Stone* that he beat me eleven games to nil.

BERNIE: Really?

ELTON: It said I got beat, which was bad enough, but since I had thrashed him it was doubly bad. That really got my back up.

BERNIE: Was that in *Rolling Stone*?

ELTON: Yes.

BERNIE: (into microphone): Hear that?

ELTON: I mean, he's amazing. Fifty city tours, you come home, and you say at the door, "Mom, I'm home," and she says, "Not today, thank you." (Laughter.) On the last American tour Larry Smith and I were holding hands on a take-off, because we both had the same sense of humor and there'd been so many crashes and hi-jacks, and he said "the engine's on fire," and I looked out the window, and it *was* on fire! He said by the end of the tour we'd be gibbering wrecks. And we were, really. I came home a wreck.

PG: In interviews over the past couple of years you've dwelled on retiring early. In one you predicted you'd retire in mid-72.

ELTON: And I'm still here! It's like Gracie Fields . . . no . . .

BERNIE: Dorothy Squires.

96

ELTON: Right. I couldn't stand the pace, if you've noticed I'm cutting down the live dates. I really do want to retire doing gigs eventually, that's what I meant. It gets to the point where your whole year is planned, you've got to do a tour of America, a tour of England, a tour of the Continent, a tour of Australia, and this year I just said, fuck it. We've never done an English tour before when we actually had a hit record out. The tour of America is going to be four or five weeks at the most, I'm not going to slog my guts out anymore. It just turns you into a moron. I'm just going to gradually cut back. I'll never ever retire from performing completely, I've become so engrossed in it. There was a bad period when I thought I couldn't take any more travelling, but now that we're cutting back I'm enjoying it. I'm gradually fading into obscurity as far as performing goes. You can't make yourself so available. It's everybody's dream to retire, whether you're a musician, or a banker, or a road sweeper. I don't think everybody relishes it in the end, though, because they're bored to tears.

PG: Do you think you could take it? Do you think you'd be bored to tears?

ELTON: I'd like to spend more time recording. But then, would the records sell if I didn't go out on the road? Am I in a strong enough position to say, I won't go out on the road, fuck it, but I will release a couple of records? Would people forget? I haven't been in the States to promote *Don't Shoot Me* and it still went to number one. I wasn't on the road to promote *Honky* and it still went to number one. I've never toured the States when I've had an album to coincide with the tour. If Donovan can do nothing for two years and then come shooting into the American charts at eighty-eight, maybe that shoots my argument down in flames. But I've always got this theory in mind that if I didn't tour, there'd be someone waiting to take my place. And would my ego stand it? I've got a tremendous ego. I'm not jealous of anybody's success, I really like to see people's success, no matter if it's with the shittiest of product, I'm really happy for them. But I've got such an ego thing now that the next record has to be as good or better and the next tour has to be better. Is there no end to it all, he said? It's probably better than having a "I don't give a fuck" attitude. So if I retired, I don't know what I'd do. If I retired tomorrow, I'd make records, I'd produce, but my ego would be deflating, and right now my ego needs inflating. It needs keeping at a certain level. I never feel as if I've really arrived. George Harrison can stay out of the public eye for two years and when his album comes out it will be an instant million-seller because everybody knows it will be good and everybody will buy it. Paul Simon, too. They've been going for so long and Elton John's been going for two and a half.

PG: If "Daniel" didn't become a bit hit in the States, would it upset you?

ELTON: I don't think it would as much as if it hadn't

98

have been a hit over here. Over here I stuck myself out on a limb and said "yes, it will be a hit." I never felt as strongly about any of our records before. "Daniel" was for me always the single, "Crocodile Rock" was just the unique thing that worked out, released to get out of the "Elton John is a slow record singer" type thinking. But in America now, a lot of people have the album, so they won't be buying the single. When I see it in the *Cashbox* Radio Active listing, having gone on all those stations, then I'll know. But I'm prepared to have a flop. I've never had a hit in this country before when I was actually here. "Crocodile" was the first one. I had this superstition that I couldn't release a record and be in the country at the same time. "Daniel" was the first one I sat trial through the whole time. I've always wanted the same respect in England I had in America. I think we've got it now, we've concentrated on England a bit more and they've responded to it.

PG: Does Bernie follow radio play of singles as closely as Elton?

BERNIE: No way. I'm always amused when he phones me up and such-and-such did a three-trillion advance or some such figure and I'll just say "is that good?"

ELTON: "Daniel" came into one of the charts at 65 the first week and he said "Oh, is that good?" He's really a dampener for the enthusiasm, Bernie is, because you'll say "fucking hell, the album went up to 91 from 176!" and he'll say "is that good?"

BERNIE: He follows the playlists and who went how

many places and who's got a bullet, that all confuses me. I look at the charts just to see if it's still on top.

ELTON: Tuesday morning when the trades come, first thing I do is look at the Radio Active list, then Kal Rudman in *Record World* and the *Billboard* album chart. Kal Rudman is really hysterical, it's like "tune in for next week's installment". For weeks and weeks he's saying such-and-such are going to be hits, and they *are*. "This record by Clint Holmes has been number one in Wichita for seven weeks and it *will* break"—and it went in the charts this week! "This record will break because it is a gorilla, a GO-RILLA!" [Everybody breaks up at Elton's accurate impersonation of Kal Rudman.]

PG: This week he's got a new category, a "creature", that's one step above Tasmanian gorilla milk.

ELTON: "This Gladys Knight album will sell over two millions units"—I mean, for an album to do over two million units is to sell a fucking lot of albums! "This is a Tasmanian GO-RILLA"—I mean, he sticks to his guns and he's right, he's amazing, but he makes such good reading, too. He's hysterical. *Record World* I like the most because they have more columns, although *Billboard* has the chit-chat column now. I love chit-chat columns. And the "Hits of the World" in *Billboard*, I look to see what's number one in Hong Kong——

BERNIE: Maxine is amazing, she looks at the trades and first thing she doesn't look at the charts to see how we're doing, she reads the gossip columns to find out who was having dinner with who at the Rainbow [in America]. "Oooh, so-and-so's going out with so-and-so!"

ELTON: I love the way the American trades never give anybody a bad review because they're afraid the advertising will be taken out. It's so hysterical. They say albums will be hits, and they've got no fucking chance. "Noddy and the Jerk-Offs on the Shit label, this is a cross between Creedence Clearwater and"— and I *believe* them and order the record and I can't wait and the fucking thing turns out to be dreadful. I *always* get hooked by those ecstatic reviews.

BERNIE: You're very gullible.

ELTON: Totally. Adverts, too.

BERNIE: I bought Bruce Springsteen just on the basis of the advert.

ELTON: I quite like that. It grows on me like the Dory Previn.

BERNIE: The worst thing about me is that I'll buy albums and put them away on the shelf and forget that I've got them.

ELTON: That's why I keep those down on the floor [points to huge piles of LPs] so I can flick through them.

BERNIE: The last three Jefferson Airplane albums were fucking horrible. I can't get into people like that anymore.

ELTON: I got a new one of theirs today.

BERNIE: All those *Sunflower* things suck——

ELTON: Well, the solo ones I never liked. [Phone rings,

101

Bernie answers.] Tell them to feed us, we're hungry.

PG: Anything you'd like to do you haven't done yet?

BERNIE: I'd like to make it with Princess Anne.

ELTON: Oh dear, oh dear, there go my connections with the Royal Family, up in flames. Actually I'd like to make a movie and show people there's more to me than meets the eye. It's got to be hilariously funny if I'm going to do it. But that's boring. Pop stars always want to make movies. What else would I like to do? I don't know. My ambitions go from day-to-day. All my childhood ambitions have been fulfilled. I'd like to see the cosmic galaxy come down into the lakes of my soda fountain water mind and live happily ever after. I'd like to win an Olympic medal, I've always admired those people.

BERNIE: The shotput. I've always wanted to be good at something like that. You do pretty well at table tennis.

ELTON: Yes, but I'd really like to win something.

PG: A Grammy? An Oscar?

ELTON: Oh, fucking things—I can launch into a tirade against those. The Grammies are a hoax. They're an insult. They're so anti-British, the Grammies. Gilbert O'Sullivan should have walked away with that fucking thing for "Alone Again (Naturally)". Instead, what wins, that bloddy "Killing"—er, "First Time Ever"—which is an English song anyway, McColl . . .

BERNIE: I hate all those award things, because they're all fixed when you get down to the people who vote for them.

102

ELTON: They're so predictable, those things. The Grammies, you knew Gilbert O'Sullivan wasn't going to get it, even though he deserved to get it. I knew Diana Ross wouldn't win an Oscar because she's black. That leaves Liza Minnelli, the sun shines out of her fucking tits.

BERNIE: That, Roger Moore, I hate him. Plastic. I hate all that. DO YOU HEAR ME? I HATE IT! (Laughter.)

ELTON: The year we were up for a Grammy at least James Taylor was up and other people like that—and the Carpenters won! The Song of the Year was "Everything Was Beautiful", Ray Stevens. I think that sums up where the Grammies are at, it's fucking disgusting. And if not "Alone Again (Naturally)", what about "American Pie?" Instead that dreary thing, and it's an old song. "Alone Again (Naturally)" is one of the great lyrics of all time. The only English people they give them to are the Beatles, and that was condescending.

BERNIE: I just hate the whole concept of starched penguins prancing around.

ELTON: They wanted me to sing at the Grammies this year. Can you imagine? Whoever sings at the Grammies or Oscars automatically goes down 5800 points because they really must be hard up. I would never sing at a record convention, that would be the most degrading thing of all-time. Apparently the year before last at the NARM convention, the rack-jobbers, they all fucking walked out on Isaac Hayes.

103

When he finished there were only fourteen people there. Rick and Pat from MCA said it was the most embarrassing thing they'd every seen. All these rack-jobbers, they're not interested in music, they're interested in how many albums they sell. Of course Isaac Hayes comes out with that black torso and Middle America goes "AAAAAAAAH!" They were all fainting, their wigs were falling off, they had to be carried out.

BERNIE: I don't mind getting a gold disc——

ELTON: Because that's actual achievement——

BERNIE: And it satisfies you. I mean, I wouldn't want to plaster my house with them.

ELTON: Thank you very much.

BERNIE: Well, at least you keep them in one room. I'd never put them in the front room, they're pretty boring.

ELTON: They've either got to go in the games room or in the toilet.

BERNIE: I mean, they are pretty boring, when you've got over six of them.

ELTON: I think they're lovely. I'd go anywhere to get a gold disc.

BERNIE: I always take them because I know in years to come I can look at them and say "You did something, Taupin."

ELTON: We got an award for the second best disco record of the year, second to Gary Glitter. You should see it, I wish they hadn't bothered. There's this thing from Australia that looks like a television

104

aerial, it's upstairs, "The King of Pop". I couldn't believe it. I was going to send it back and ask who was "The Queen of Lemonade". It's all given good-heartedly, but ... shit ... unless you've actually achieved something ...

PG: How would you feel about a BMI certificate?

ELTON: That's even worse. Ask me how I feel about BMI.

PG: How do you feel about BMI, Elton?

ELTON: I love ASCAP.

BERNIE: What do you mean, a BMI certificate? Who's going to give me a "BMI Certificate"?

ELTON: We've already got one, for "Your Song". They're boring, they're really boring.

BERNIE: Well, who needs that? I'd rather have a shellacked American chart with our album at number one than some bit of shitty parchment that says you've written a good song. Who are they? They don't know what's a good song.

ELTON: Songs of the Year—I mean, it's like the Eurovision Song Contest.

BERNIE: The Eurovision Song Contest is really a contest to pick the worst song in Europe.

ELTON: It's quite comical. Did you watch last Saturday when they had ...

BERNIE: Where they had the different people? Oh, some of them were amazing!

ELTON: There was this couple from Belgium that couldn't have been living for the last ten years.

BERNIE: You mean the Unisex couple? That went—

[Elton and Bernie proceed to do their routine] I mean, she had peroxide blonde hair and a huge nose and he had an ill-fitting toupee.

ELTON: It's called "Baby, Baby. Baby", the song. That part of show biz I hate. Not the part that's Katherine Hepburn, Groucho Marx—they've got style, they've got panache, they don't give a fuck about anything, they just rise above it. I've always hoped I could rise above it. I've never been able to understand anybody who thinks Tony Bennett is good.

BERNIE: I can't understand anybody who thinks that Tony Bennett can *sing*. He's got to have the most boring, monotonous, tuneless voice——

ELTON: Anybody like that, shouldn't just pick on Tony Bennett, poor chap, because he's got a big nose, but the only person I can tolerate is Sinatra. That side of the business really depresses me. I can't see how anybody can get pleasure out of singing songs like "In Our Mountain Greenery" or "The Look of Love".

BERNIE: It's so false, so predictable.

ELTON: They come out on stage in their fucking dresses and their bee-hive hairdos and get a standing ovation.

BERNIE: People actually sit there and say "wow, doesn't he sing that with so much feeling."

ELTON: I suppose Streisand stands out——

BERNIE: She has class.

ELTON: I'd rather hear Lou Reed or Leonard Cohen sing any day than Andy Williams or Tony Bennett. I mean, Andy Williams is a nice guy, I can tolerate him because he at least owns up, but Tony Bennett really

106

believes it. That side of the business, I can't believe it exists! I can understand our parents liking it, because it was the era they grew up in, the dance band era, but some kids of our age actually like it. They actually like James Last and Ray Coniff.

BERNIE: I can't understand people buying records of hits sung by other people. Those things like you used to do.

ELTON: But they sell *massively*. The mass of this country must be morons. I really believe I have more talent in my little finger than Tony Bennett or anybody like that can ever possibly hope to achieve in a life-time. Someone might say, "alright, why did you do the Royal Variety Show?" We did the Royal Variety Show, but we did a sort of rebellion, Larry threw the farting balloons and tap-danced away and I sang "I Think I'm Gonna Kill Myself", which I thought was quite an achievement to get allowed in. But I never ever want to stoop to the level of that other part of show business.

BERNIE: Elton, I'm starving.

PG: So are we, actually.

ELTON: Well, Bernie, there's this fish-and-chips take-out in the village. You can't miss it. Here, this should cover it. You're the only one here with a car at the moment. [Ten minutes later we were all dining on cod and chips.]

ONE
YEAR
ON

(This conversation was recorded exactly one year to the day after the rest of this book. Elton was speaking in the Rocket offices.)

PG: *Yellow Brick Road* has stayed in the US top ten for half a year.

ELTON: It *is* weird. When it came out I was paranoid, about it being a double album. Again, shows you how much I know, I wanted to release it as two singles. I got talked out of it by America. That album is going to be hard to follow up, even though we've finished the next album. It's just one of those albums which is going to keep going, especially when the documentary is shown in the States in May. The album went from eleven to number one over here after going down, so it will probably help the album again. It could be around for ages. I'm not complaining, but things like that happen in the States, don't they? Charlie Rich was around for awhile before it broke, Maria Muldaur is climbing the charts now, and John Denver is storming up there.

PG: How would you describe the next album?

ELTON: There are no strings on it whatsoever, I think it's the first album ever done without any strings. Del

Newman did a French horn arrangement on "Don't Let the Sun Go Down", which is probably the strongest candidate for a single. Again, I don't know, because if it were up to me my career would probably be down there by now. There are about 3 tracks that could definitely be singles, and will be, probably one is "The Bitch is Back", which was going to be the title for awhile but then everyone might think I was jumping on the glam rock bandwagon. Boring!

PG: How long before you finish your commitment to Dick James?

ELTON: We're possibly recording the Festival Hall concert, we're going to go back and do lots of old numbers, which is the only way you can really do a live album, is a mixture of old and new. If we were recording the gigs we do now it would be basically the stuff off the last three albums. We couldn't issue that as a live album. We've got two studio albums and a "Floater", which can either be a live album or a Best Of. After the one we do in August there'll be another one, which we do next January. Then he can do whatever he wants with the old masters, unless we buy them back, which is very, very unlikely. You may find the DJM equivalent of Music For Pleasure Elton John . . .

PG: Have you been approached by different record companies?

ELTON: Everbody. You name it. Everybody, everybody, literally. We haven't really sat down and talked seriously with anybody yet, but we've had approaches. It was exactly the same with the publishing. I don't think we'll even start talking until later on in the year. I think MCA have done a good job on the album and the single, which has been a lesson for them. To see "Bennie and the Jets" go in the soul chart is a new experience for them.

PG: You've been so busy, the recording must have been gruelling.

ELTON: It was gruelling because I don't think an album has ever been made under such intense pressure, not one of our albums, anyway. We'd just done a gruelling American and English tour and just had a little relief at Christmas, and then gone straight over to Denver. We had a few hassles to start with, we couldn't get used to the monitoring system. I always do terrible moodies at the start of albums. I went through a weird one after writing all the songs so we lost three days of recording. We'd only booked ten, because that's all it usually takes. So we did two backing tracks in one day and then literally did twelve in the next 3. Everybody was feeling very tired and irritable, and the thought of going to Japan and Australia for a month or so was just killing everybody. Everybody was fatigued during the album, after the album and during the tour. We came off the road in New Zealand at a peak because we knew that we'd all agreed, after four years we were just going to have a rest. We were getting like robots again. And when Ray Cooper joined as a percussionist it was always under the impression that he would eventually get to do something else, so if we had continued with the tour we would never have the chance to rehearse with him on organ or sax or whatever he's going to play. So we're going to rehearse and try to get some new things, to experiment, because I don't think you can stand still. We can't improve on the way we are now with Ray on percussion, so the time has come for me to get off my big fat ass. I asked the band about him ages ago, and they said, yes, it would be a good idea. Blue Mink had just got him out of doing session work and onto the road, he'd never been on the road before. They were his friends because they were all more or less session musicians, so he said I'll have to stay with them, so I said we'll wait, and after we came back from America I phoned him up and Blue Mink were more or less breaking up. He said yes, and that was it. He was the only person I really wanted to add, and we had to wait for about ten months.

PG: What's on the album besides "The Bitch Is Back"?

ELTON: There's a song called "Grimsby" which I suggested more than usual, because I usually never suggest anything to Bernie. Randy Newman did a song called "Cleveland", so I thought we should do the English equivalent. The Beatles did a medley with a nonsense Italian thing on *Abbey Road*, so Bernie wrote a song with different words that just meant nothing, which obviously we're going to be a prime target for. Bernie wrote "Solar Prestige A Gammon", which I sing in an Italian accent. "Don't Let the Sun" is, again, a sad love song. "Pinkie" is a very happy love song, "Bitch is Back" is a rock-and-roller, "You're So Static" is sort of a send-up of groovy trendy American ladies. It's a rock-and-roll song. "Ticking" is probably the deepest lyric he's ever written. It's a pretty song, and he'll probably come under the same criticism he did for "Indian Sunset". I don't think it's pretentious, it's just a very heavy lyric. There's a couple of country-and-western tracks. We did fourteen, it's just a matter of whittling down, I think there'll be about nine. We don't have anything lying around, we use them as B-sides or as two B-sides.

PG: Do you feel odd coming back to this office after a tour?

ELTON: I always feel guilty because I'm rushing in and out instead of spending a whole day. You can't just walk in and say "That's wrong," because you don't work in the atmosphere. I don't want to work here anyway. I want to listen to things, and do some more things with Kiki. It was a mish-mosh the way "Hard Luck Story" was done, I had to mix it in Colorado and you always want to hear a mix in more than one studio. I got disappointed because of the reaction to it, people saying she should stick to ballads, because I think they're wrong. I don't think it's harmed her. I think she's better off doing her own songs anyway, Bernie and I have been responsible for writing two of her flops.

PG: How does London strike you on return?

ELTON: I honestly feel there's more happening in America now than in England. Not just in music, in fashion, anything. Especially in Los Angeles, which is so laid back that many musicians are just saying "Get on with it!" It's so hard for groups to make it over here, they've got nothing to help them. Every single factor is against them: the price of going on the road, the cost of getting equipment, petrol, getting records played on the radio over here is impossible. At least groups in the States can actually get FM airplay. Over here it's terrible, I think it's disgusting.

PG: You had an experience with John Lennon in L.A., didn't you?

ELTON: It was very embarrassing. You come out of Los Angeles Airport after one of those Jumbo flights, and there are millions of people there waiting to see their relations, and I couldn't see anybody there to meet me. I said, this is terrible, there's nobody here, and all of a sudden I hear "No, no, it's him, it's him, it's Elton!" Lennon was on the floor, I said "Oh, shit!" It was great fun, but at the time everyone was highly embarrassed. I love John, I think he's amazing.

PG: Even though you cancelled the European tour, you're doing the Watford fund-raiser.

ELTON: I also did three benefits this week for Watford, the coach and two players, on my own, just me and a piano singing "Saturday Night's Alright for Fighting", which is very strange. I really enjoyed it. But I promised them so long ago there was no way I could cancel things like that. The charity things we promised to do will be honored.

Football is relaxation for me. I just love it, I really missed it when I was away. I just enjoy football.

It's a drag the European tour was cancelled, because if anything's cancelled it's usually Europe that suffers. But it's always been easy for me to agree to do something like that six months in advance. I think it's up to me now not to agree to anything that's too far ahead in the future.

THE ALBUMS OF ELTON JOHN

Empty Sky	DJLPS	403
Elton John	DJLPS	406
Tumbleweed Connection	DJLPS	410
17-11-70	DJLPS	414
Madman Across the Water	DJLPH	420
Honky Chateau	DJLPH	423
Don't Shoot Me, I'm Only the Piano Player	DJLPH	427
Goodbye Yellow Brick Road	DJLPD	1001
Caribou	Summer 1974	

THE SINGLES OF ELTON JOHN

Title	DJM UK number	US label & number	Highest BBC position	Highest US position	Release month
Lady Samantha	BF 1739	Unreleased			Jan 69
It's Me That You Need	DJS 205	Unreleased			May 69
Border Song	DJS 217	Uni 55246		92	March 70
Rock and Roll Madonna	DJS 222	Unreleased			June 70
Your Song	DJS 237	Uni 55265	7	8	Jan 71
Friends	DJS 244	Uni 55277		34	April 71
Levon	Unreleased	Uni 55314		24	Dec 71
Tiny Dancer	Unreleased	Uni 55318		41	March 72

Rocket Man	DJX 501	Uni 55328	2	April 72
Honky Cat	DJS 269	Uni 55343	31	Aug 72
Crocodile Rock	DJS 271	MCA 40000	2	Oct 72
Daniel	DJS 275	MCA 40046	4	Jan 73
Saturday Night's Alright				
For Fighting	DJX 502	MCA 40105	7	June 73
Goodbye Yellow Brick Road	DJS 285	MCA 40148	6	Sept 73
Step Into Christmas	DJS 290	MCA 65108	24	Nov 73
Candle in the Wind	DJS 297	Unreleased	11	Feb 74
Bennie and the Jets	DJS 297	MCA 40198	1	Feb 74

When no chart position is indicated, the record did not achieve a chart position. Release dates refer to British release, which usually antedated American release, except in the cases of "Levon" and "Tiny Dancer", which were only available in the UK on *Madman Across the Water*.

If you have enjoyed this book see also further titles
in the

STAR BOOKS
MUSIC SERIES

JIMI HENDRIX
by Curtis Knight   *60p Illustrated*

BURIED ALIVE
The story of Janis Joplin
by Myra Friedman   *65p Illustrated*

THE ROLLING STONES
An Unauthorised Biography
edited by David Dalton   *65p Illustrated*

THE NEW MUSICAL EXPRESS
BOOK OF ROCK
edited by Nick Logan and
Rob Finnis   *50p Illustrated*

THE GRATEFUL DEAD
edited by Hank Harrison   *60p Illustrated*

THE COASTERS
by Bill Millar   *60p Illustrated*

All prices are subject to change. See the final page of this
book for our availability guide.

JIMI
HENDRIX

Curtis Knight

This is the full and dramatic story of the life, work, and death of Hendrix — the superstar who scorched a trail to a new and stormy high for his myriads of fanatical disciples. Curtis Knight, friend and fellow musician, takes us through the scene. Hard times, good times, money, managers, drugs, groupies, girlfriends, hopes, dreams . . . and finally death. It is the definitive biography, the last word on a great musician.   *60p Illustrated*

BURIED ALIVE

The Story of Janis Joplin
Myra Friedman

For those who loved her rich raucous sound and for those who never heard her sing a single note, BURIED ALIVE is a biography (written by a professional associate and close friend) which will touch the heart. For Janis's life is the stuff of great biography. She was a lonely, insecure woman whose suicidal life-style brought her immense adulation, wealth and sometimes happiness, but left her dead. This is also the story of the crazy, violent, electric, sexy sixties, which Janis embodied and which she barely saw through.

65p Illustrated

THE
ROLLING
STONES

An Unauthorised Biography
edited by David Dalton

From the earliest beginnings David Dalton has captured that illusive, aggressive personality that was the core of the Stones' music and the life-style of this the greatest rock n' roll band in the world. Interviews, articles, film and record reviews, a day-to-day diary of events now an integral part of rock history, magnificent pictures spanning the band's career, and a full discography from both sides of the Atlantic. A mass of inside information and entertainment.   *65p Illustrated*

THE NEW MUSICAL EXPRESS BOOK OF ROCK

edited by Nick Logan and Rob Finnis

A kaleidoscope of rich information from the annals of that bestselling music magazine. An entertaining documentation of the acts which form the core of rock in the seventies, those on the periphery whose contribution is valid however small, and those whose groundwork back in the fifties and sixties made the development of today's rock 'n' roll possible. Interlaced with all the main entries are fascinating definitions of some of the rock terms in current usage, e.g. accapella, feedback, punk-rock, along with the addresses for the major record companies and premier rock venues. Plus, of course, a mass of exclusive photographs. *50p Illustrated*

THE GRATEFUL DEAD

edited by Hank Harrison

San Francisco had just produced the Kerouac and Ginsberg and Ferlinghetti phalanx and New York the abstract expressionists. Now it was Music's turn. Suddenly everyone knew the musicians were the oracles and the fonts of life. Just as suddenly The Grateful Dead was born. This is their story in words and pictures. It is the story of an era that brought meaning and life to a whole new generation. *60p Illustrated*

THE COASTERS

Bill Millar

This is the incredible story of how two Jewish teenagers
from the North-East and a number of black singers from
the South met up in Los Angeles and began to change the
world of Music beyond recognition. Slowly and inexcrably,
with such classics as YAKETY YAK, SWEET GEORGIA
BROWN, SEARCHIN', POISON IVY, and CHARLIE
BROWN, they eradicated the music colour line. Few then
realised that R&B would become so dominant a facet of
Western culture. This book examines, through their
personalities and careers, the very considerable part The
Coasters and Lieber and Stoller played in that enormous
cultural growth. Bill Millar is the author of THE
DRIFTERS.   *60p Illustrated*